The Digest Book Of
DOG CARE

Edited by Susan Bernstein

DBI BOOKS, INC., NORTHFIELD, ILL.

ISBN 0-695-81289-0   **Library of Congress Catalog Card #79-50063**

CONTENTS

INTRODUCTION

Why Own a Dog? 5

Chapter 1: DAY-TO-DAY CARE

The New Arrival 8

Training Your Dog for Home Living 11

Routine Health Care 14

Exercise 17

Regular Grooming 19

The Bath 22

Chapter 2: TRAINING

Housebreaking 25

Special Training 27

Dog Training Tips 29

Heel 30

Down 32

Sit 34

Stay 36

Come 38

Chapter 3: FEEDING

A Dog's Dietary Needs 41

Special Feeding 44

Digestive Problems 47

Feeding Fallacies 48

Chapter 4: HEALTH

Health Guide 50
Some Orthopedic Problems 62
Other Health Hints 63
Knowing What's Normal is Vital 65
Beware of Accidental Poisoning 66
Dogs in Wintertime 66
Problems of Old Age 68
First Aid Chart 70

Chapter 5: BREEDING/PREGNANCY/PUPPIES

Should You Breed Your Dog? 73
The Breeding Process 74
Pregnancy 77
The Puppies 83
Causes of Puppy Deaths 86
Weaning 89

Chapter 6: SHOWING

Showing Your Dog 94

WHY OWN A DOG?

THAT'S really a good question. Why own a dog? Who needs it? Why take on another responsibility, another mouth to feed, another complication, another source of concern, another burden? Life is complex enough, why add another element to an already over-taxed situation? A dog may create spots on your carpeting, possibly tear your drapes, chew your furniture, scratch up your woodwork, ruin your lawn, disrupt your peace and quiet, and occasionally cause friction with your neighbors. So who needs that? Or what about those sudden urgent outings in the midst of a blizzard or late at night when you would rather go directly to sleep or at ten in the morning when you intended to sleep until noon? All those expenses too—vet, license, shots, stitches after a dog fight, X-rays for that swallowed bone, kennel fees while you're away—and on and on. Who needs it? What about all the extra work—brushing, bathing, feeding, and walking? Non-dog owners ask these kinds of questions and they do so in all sincerity for they truly cannot understand the whole bit.

We, who keep and love dogs, often merely smile knowingly and don't try to refute such arguments. Others, who are patient and understanding, may try to explain to the non-believer what we, in the dog fancy, know so well: that the love and companionship of a dog is one of the truly satisfying, rewarding, enjoyable, enriching, fulfilling, and unforgettable relationships one can have in life. Picture what a marvelous experience it is to be always welcomed by an excited, loving, tail-wagging friend. It's incredibly emotionally uplifting to be greeted with such warmth and love when returning home from the alien outside world. What a rare situation to have someone give you lifelong, non-diminishing, unaltered love; with so little demanded in return. Once a dog's confidence and affection is won, it is for life. The loyalty dogs display is quite remarkable. Innumerable stories have been told which illustrate the tremendous loyalty and love of dogs. We know of dogs who traveled hundreds of miles to find their master, or those who sacrificed their lives to remain with or to rescue their master. The news media regularly recounts tales of dog heroism—rescuing a drowning person, saving someone from a flaming building, warning of danger and attacking an intruder.

In this highly computerized, mechanized, data processed, and impersonal world, there is a comforting sensation in sharing your abode with something that is still very natural. This need felt by modern man has resulted in the tremendous growth of pet ownership. Man apparently needs and appreciates this type of relationship—providing for an animal's existence in return for its love. The animal pet which is capable of actually offering the most in return is the dog.

Dogs have been man's companion and helper since ancient times. Art and literature testifies to this fact. Through the ages, dogs have remained with man during good times as well as bad. Dogs were the first domesticated animals and originally won man over by proving their usefulness. Scientists believe that dogs served first as scavengers, thus keeping their masters' camping site clean. Later, they proved themselves by herding, being beasts of burden, and assistants in hunting. Even today, numerous breeds of dogs serve man. Yet most dogs, even though they may have a definite working role, will also be a faithful companion to the one they serve.

Love, loyalty, companionship are the basic ingredients in the man-dog relationship, as well as the dog's unquestioning subservience. When you have your dog at your side you need never feel alone. In fact, this truth is being more fully realized today than

---

REASONS FOR THE PET BOOM

- More leisure time and an affluent society are the reasons most often given for the growth of interest in pets. Certainly the increase in the number of registered, pure-bred dogs (about 7 per cent a year since 1958) substantiates this theory.
- Parents perennially give children pets for their educational value.
- Many people these days are acquiring dogs for protection as well as companionship.
- New thinking among psychologists offers the theory that *people need pets*. A leading exponent of this theory, Dr. Boris Levinson, Professor of Psychology at Yeshiva University and a clinical psychotherapist, says this in his new book *Pet-Oriented Child Psychotherapy*.
  Pet Food Institute

ever before. Many institutions have come to realize the positive value of dogs and have begun utilizing them for therapy. Institutions for the mentally disturbed have discovered the beneficial aspects of dogs through controlled experiments and found that their patients responded well to these pets. Some psychiatrists are using animals, dogs in particular, in working with disturbed children. Senior citizens find tremendous comfort in their dogs and some keep going because of them.

Probably the only real disappointment experienced by the dog owner is the loss of this close, beloved companion. Since the dog's life span is shorter, man outlives his canine friend. However, since replacement is quite easy, this loss can become the opportunity for making a new relationship. Each animal is unique in its own way, but yet they can all provide the love and companionship, fun and frolic, that we all desire.

In today's crime ridden society, dog ownership is growing because people wish to use them as a deterrent. Research has shown that a large dog, for example, will do a good job of guarding since its presence alone scares off undesirable characters. Even a small dog can serve a valuable guarding function by merely being alert enough to bark at an intruder, since noise will often discourage them.

Why own a dog? Has the question been answered? Perhaps words cannot truly explain this phenomenon. But, if you are willing to take some chances, overlook some little "accidents," devote a little time and effort, you will be amazed by the rewards to be reaped. To our knowledge, there have been few real regrets by those who make the final plunge and adopt a dog. Errors in selection and judgment do occur, but these can be corrected. Therefore, don't let fear of a mistake be a deterrent. Dog ownership isn't like marriage or like having a child. Should you be unhappy with your new dog and it's something that can't be worked out, then do exchange him for another. Amazingly, such a problem is rather infrequent. Most people are delighted with their four-footed, furry selection.

DAY-TO-DAY CARE

THE NEW ARRIVAL

For housebreaking purposes keep the puppy confined to an area that is easy to keep clean and yet where "socialization" is possible as well. (Ericonji Basenjis, Northbrook, Illinois.)

A dog needs to have his own bed and a spot he can consider his own. The bed need not be fancy, just suitable in size and easy to keep clean. (Photo by Maria Coven.)

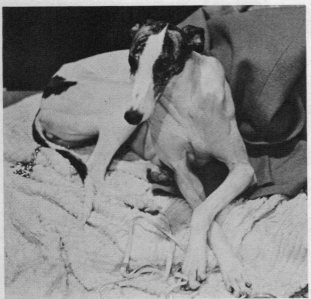

WHAT an exciting moment it is when you've made your selection and that darling, warm, lovable new dog is ready and waiting to enter your home and your life. A young puppy will need certain essentials, and pre-planning should make it an enjoyable rather than a hectic experience. *A small box,* lined with newspapers, is needed for transporting your new possession. Place the box on the back floor of the car so that the dog will be secure. If you have a long ride home from the breeder, stop occasionally so the puppy can relieve himself. Since this is undoubtedly his first car ride, he may be nervous and need reassurance. Allow him to have water only if the trip is long or very hot. Normally, it is best not to feed a puppy just prior to, or during, an automobile ride as this can induce car sickness.

Once you arrive home, get the dog settled with a minimum of fuss and excitement. His living "area" should have been selected and readied in advance. In most homes or apartments, the kitchen is the ideal spot to confine the puppy until housebreaking is completed. We recommend an area which is both easy to keep clean and where the puppy will be near you and have "human contact." *Socialization is most important, so the puppy should not be isolated.* Some dog trainers recommend a wire cage but if there is an alternative which would give the dog somewhat more freedom and yet keep it confined to a specific area, this is ideal.

Don't give your puppy free run of the house. Training cannot be accomplished if this is done.

The Bed

Provide your dog with his own bed and place it in one corner of his area. The bed should be appropriate to the dog's size—cozy enough to cuddle in. Most breeds will outgrow their first bed, so it should be

Puppy Training Tip

Keeping a new puppy in a playpen for a few days will protect him from overenthusiastic hugging by the children and may also save rugs and furniture from accidents. Chicken wire stapled to the outside of playpen frame will keep a small dog inside. With a blanket for his bed, some toys, and newspapers over the playpen floor, he'll soon begin to paper-train himself.

BEFORE THE DOG ARRIVES

When a dog enters the family circle for the first time, certain adjustments and plans need to be made beforehand. Responsibilities must be clearly defined. The dog's feeding, grooming, and training must be provided for. Who will do these chores and when they will do them must be spelled out. Remember, the well being of an animal is too important to be entrusted solely to a youngster; close adult supervision is necessary.

If family members are going to be away, arrangements for the care of the puppy must be made. The dog cannot be left alone for an extended period, especially when it is still on three meals per day. Someone must be able to come in and care for the pup. Arranging for a "puppy sitter" is a good idea. That way, the dog can be fed and taken out and a regular schedule maintained.

inexpensive. A small washable rug or blanket can be used. Frequent washing of the bedding is necessary.

Newspaper

Stock up on newspapers since you will be using large quantities if you "paper train" your puppy.

Dishes

Your dog will need two dishes, one for his food and one for water. Dishes which are unbreakable, weighted and rustproof are best. You will find a weighted dish is worth the extra cost in order to avoid spilled water and food. Puppies love to play and will run around and frolic with an aluminum or small plastic container. And it's amazing, but, until the family members are fully adjusted to the new addition and all his equipment, they will accidentally tip over the water dish—unless it is weighted. The size and shape of the dishes should be determined by the size and shape of the dog's head and ears. Dogs with long ears should have a dish with a narrow opening so that their ears stay out of the food. Flat-faced dogs need a shallow dish and long-nosed dogs need a deep bowl.

The shape of the dog's feeding dish is determined by the shape of the nose and length of the ears. This long nosed Pointer would enjoy a deep bowl. (Photo courtesy of American Field.)

Health

Visit your veterinarian and have him give the puppy a complete checkup. Be certain the dog is healthy and sound, because, if something is wrong, it would be best to return him now before getting attached. Bring a stool sample to the vet so he can check for worms. Any innoculations needed can be given at this time.

Other Essentials

A small collar and a leash will have to be purchased. The size and shape should be suitable to the dog. For example, a rounded collar is used for a long haired dog so that it won't rub off the fur. Again, as this item also will soon be outgrown, an inexpensive one is best.

Puppies love to chew and unless you provide them with something to gnaw on, they will help themselves. Don't ever allow them to chew an old shoe or sock, because a dog can't discriminate between one of your "good" shoes and an old one. Do provide your puppy with rawhide bones which are made specifically for this chewing purpose. They can be purchased at pet stores or wherever dog food is sold. Avoid rubber or plastic toys as these can be chewed to pieces and can lodge in the dog's throat or digestive tract, causing severe damage and even death.

A Reminder

Don't forget to purchase a dog license promptly or to comply immediately with local rules on rabies innoculation and other shots.

Grooming Materials

To keep your puppy looking neat and clean, you will need a suitable brush, comb, and nail clippers. The type of comb and brush required will depend on the dog's coat and even his size, so discuss this at time of purchase. Don't get carried away with enthusiasm and purchase large amounts of grooming equipment and aids. Comb, brush, and nail clippers are the basic essentials. A mild dog shampoo is also needed. Other items can be purchased when you discover a real need.

Diet

Since moving to a new home is quite traumatic for a dog and just this change can cause digestive disturbances, it is wise to maintain the dog's former diet. Once your puppy has adjusted to your home and his digestion is normal, you may wish to start a different diet. We would recommend discussing the maintenance diet with your vet and planning one that is suitable to the breed, the activity level of your dog, and one that will help him attain optimum growth and development.

The First Nights

The first few nights the puppy spends in his new home are the most difficult. He misses the warmth and companionship of his brothers, sisters, and mother. Most puppies will cry, but comforting words, a little petting, a hot water bottle, and a ticking clock will ease the anxious baby. Remember a puppy is a baby dog, and he will often require nearly as much attention as a new infant. You should plan to devote a few days to this baby and to making him feel at home; however, don't spoil him and start bad habits. It is a sad mistake to let him sleep in your room and bed. Once this is started, your privacy is over. The dog should have his own bed in a cozy nook in another part of the house and sleep there without exception. This procedure should be followed from the beginning.

Let the puppy sleep when he wants to. Don't start off by having numerous visitors come over to see him and pick him up. A gradual introduction to the family members is wise. Small puppies must be handled with utmost care. Children and many adults must be taught how to pick them up, hold them, carry them, and put them down. Injuring a small pup by careless treatment is cruel and needless.

Until the puppy has had all his shots and innoculations, it is best to keep him away from other dogs in order to avoid unnecessary exposure to disease.

TRAINING YOUR DOG FOR HOME LIVING

Psychology of Dog Care

AS you will soon discover, a dog that is intended as a house pet quickly becomes a family member. Since he will, hopefully, be living happily with you for a number of years, it is a wise and necessary thing for you to guide him into acceptable behavior. A dog must learn to conform to your life style and not vice versa, thus standards should be set from the very beginning. Be certain that all the members of the family understand what these standards are, and that all abide by them. It is most important to be consistent so that the dog will not be confused.

Virtually all dogs like to please their master and once they fully understand what is required of them, and how to do it, they will. Therefore, it is most desirable to develop a sense of affection and companionship between master and dog. Training is easier and more fun once this relationship is established. The dog is truly man's best friend—he will be loyal and faithful. It's nice to be able to feel deserving of this devotion.

Training for Everyday Living

When bringing home a new dog, be he young or old, you must begin training immediately. Show him what he can and cannot do—where he can go and cannot go—and sometimes when and with whom things are or are not permissable. If there is a room or even parts of the house that you don't want him to enter, then establish that from the beginning and be firm about it. Be consistent, don't allow him to enter the room on one day and then punish him the next. The first lesson to teach a dog is what you mean by saying "NO." Make this your first training lesson. Once he learns this, all other lessons become easier. How can this be done? Put a special tidbit down and when he goes for it, yell "No" and slap him away. Keep repeating this procedure until the pup stops approaching the tidbit. When you put down his food dish, say "No" and make him wait until you are ready for him to eat. *Repetition, firmness,* and *reward* will do the trick. Try to always reward your dog when he responds correctly by giving him a dog treat or something special he likes and training will be easier and faster.

Your dog can be taught to do the following:

(1) To Behave While You Are Eating
No "begging at the table" can be accomplished simply by never giving the dog anything to eat from the table. And if he should beg, firmly say "no" and push or send him away. Keeping him away from your eating area until he gets the message will also help. Dogs that beg at the table frequently do so because, at first, they were allowed to or even encouraged. When the owner later decides that this is annoying and should stop, it is very difficult to "unlearn" this bad behavior.

(2) To Stay off Furniture
From earliest puppyhood, teach your dog his restrictions. You may enjoy having your St. Bernard puppy on the couch, but consider what this will mean when he grows up. So, don't allow your pup to do anything you wouldn't allow your fully grown

---

THE DO'S AND DON'TS OF DOG OWNERSHIP

DON'T . . .
- let your dog roam the neighborhood
- let your dog bark excessively
- let your dog soil your neighbor's shrubbery or lawn, or tear up his flower garden
- let your dog chase cars or bicycles
- let your dog frighten or bite the postman, milkman, or other service people
- let your leashed dog lunge at or jump on passers-by
- let your dog howl for hours while you are gone

DO . . .
- teach your dog to be obedient and well-behaved
- walk your dog on a leash and curb him when necessary
- teach him to stay in your yard
- train your dog to stay quietly within his kennel or crate while you are away
- train your dog to walk quietly at heel on a loose leash

*Don't ever allow your puppy on the furniture unless
you want him to be there when he grows up.*

*Your puppy needs to be trained to walk on the leash.
This is not instinctive.*

dog. If you don't want him on your furniture, **never**
allow him to be on it!

(3) Not to Run Out the Door

For city and suburban dwellers this is a most important lesson. Too many dogs are lost or run over and injured or killed by automobiles. Make this lesson one of your first and most important ones and be sure it is learned well. Even if your yard is fenced in or if you live far from the road, train your dog to go out only when you give your permission. If your facilities are not enclosed, train your dog never to go out the door without the leash and you. This training is best accomplished while the puppy is still small. Running out at mailmen and delivery men is a very popular canine sport but this very disturbing behavior should not be permitted to become a habit.

(4) To Walk on the Leash

Have your new puppy wear a small collar. When he becomes accustomed to having it on—this may take several days — attach a leash and let him walk around with it on. Then, gradually begin holding it and walking with him. Don't pull or drag him, just gently guide him until he becomes accustomed to responding to the lead. Don't allow the pup to bite the leash or to tangle himself around your legs. Speak to him, be friendly but firm, and reward him with praising and petting when he does it correctly.

(5) Not to Bark Unnecessarily

Most people want their dog to bark when a stranger is around or in case of some danger. However, too many dogs bark constantly at people or events, and this becomes annoying and bothersome. So, if your dog barks when you leave the house, you must return and scold him. Barking at mailmen, delivery men, and garbage men must also be curtailed early. Shout "No," clamp the mouth shut with your hand, and swat the behind with a rolled-up newspaper. Splashing them with cold water or picking them up and shaking them soundly while scolding has also been suggested. Be persistent and consistent.

It is most disturbing to your neighbors if your dog barks while outside; don't allow this. If he persists in barking, act firmly. Some authorities suggest throwing a bucket of water on the dog that barks in the yard, while others suggest using a spray attachment on the garden hose. Punish him immediately when he barks and he will soon understand that this is unacceptable behavior.

(6) Not to Chew and Tear Clothes or Furniture
Never give the puppy an old shoe, sock, or piece of clothing with which to play for it is impossible for him to distinguish between a shoe he may chew and one he isn't allowed to touch. A pup has a strong natural chewing instinct. He needs to chew to ease some of the discomfort of teething and to keep himself occupied. Give him rawhide bones to chew— these are healthy and won't cause you any damage. For safety, once the pieces get small, take them away as a small piece of rawhide can be swallowed and get stuck in the puppy's throat.

If junior chews at furniture punish him immediately with a good hard slap and tie him up or confine him to a place where he can't do any harm. Chewing can be a very expensive and destructive habit if allowed to continue. Remember that a small destructive dog will mature and become even more destructive. If you find you can't control the situation, don't delay —call a professional trainer for assistance.

(7) Not to Snap, Growl, or Bite
Instinctively, most dogs will growl if anyone approaches them while they are eating or gnawing on a bone. Some will snap and even bite if their food is touched. Such behavior must not be tolerated. Demonstrate to your dog that you can and will take his food dish or bone away from him and don't tolerate any signs of anger from him. You may have to do some punishing, but it's easier to do this with a young puppy than to have a mean, full grown dog who can't be approached while eating.

Dog License

In most parts of the United States, it is required that you get your dog licensed. These license fees are an excise tax levied upon the dogs of the community or county. License-issuing agencies are required to keep dog records and to supply the dog owner with a license tag. This tag is designed to be placed on a dog's collar. It serves to identify the dog if he is picked up by police. But it also identifies him if he gets lost. So a dog license tag is good insurance for you. Remember, the tag is no good to you unless it is securely fastened to the dog's collar, and the dog must be wearing that collar.

Training for Everyday Living
A new dog should be taught the do's and don'ts that constitute acceptable behavior. As soon as possible teach your dog the following:
- To Behave While You Are Eating
- To Stay Off Furniture
- Not to Run Out the Door
- To Walk on the Leash
- Not to Bark Unnecessarily
- Not to Chew and Tear Clothes or Furniture
- Not to Snap, Growl or Bite

Unnecessary barking is very annoying—train your dog in proper canine behavior.

A vicious dog is a frightening thing—from earliest puppyhood your dog must be taught not to snap, growl, or bite.

13

ROUTINE HEALTH CARE

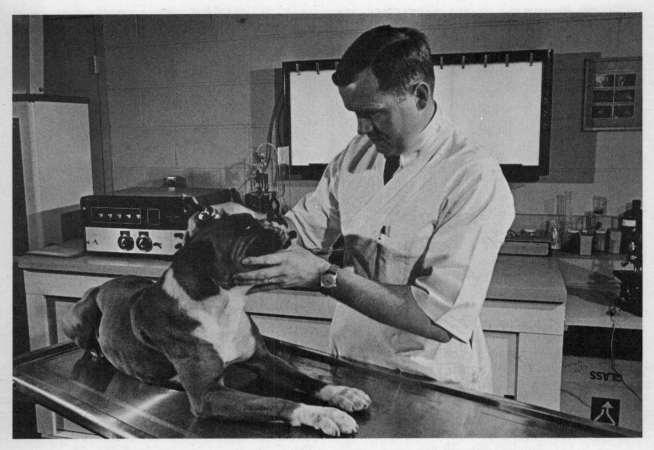

Your veterinarian uses all the knowledge and tools of modern medicine to keep your pet in good health. (Dr. Tom Keefe—Purina Pet Care Center.)

AN integral part of the care of your family dog is regular veterinary visits. During puppyhood, the visits will be quite frequent as all the necessary innoculations must be taken promptly. Distemper, leptospirosis and hepatitis can now be practically prevented by the proper administration of vaccines. Although they are not 100 per cent effective, the incidence of these dread diseases has been significantly reduced. Your veterinarian will work out a schedule of innoculations for your new puppy and will advise you about yearly booster shots. Since there is now a triple booster covering these diseases, one booster injection is all that is necessary. The innoculation for rabies should also be given during the first year and then repeated yearly. Many communities make this yearly rabies vaccination mandatory.

It is good preventative medicine to have the vet check your dog at least once a year—when you go in for boosters. Ask him to check your dog's teeth and gums and to remove tartar accumulations. If you have the slightest suspicion that your dog may have worms, then have the vet examine a stool specimen.

There are many things which should be done at home as part of your routine health care program:

(1) Maintain a clean environment: wash the dog's bedding frequently, wash the eating utensils scrupulously after each meal, provide fresh water daily.

(2) Protect your pet from unnecessary dangers: train him to stay off the street, keep your garbage cans covered, remove him when insecticides and other poisons are being used.

(3) Be perceptive: take note of changes in your

dog's appetite, digestion, and personality.

(4) Examine your dog at every grooming: observe any skin lesions and treat accordingly; check eyes, ears and feet. Run your hands over the body checking for tumors.

Should your dog be ill and require treatment, be sure you follow the vet's directions carefully and administer medication only as directed. Provide as quiet and restful an environment for your sick pet as possible. Your care and love will help to speed his recovery.

Care of the Female

The ownership of an unspayed female presents certain responsibilities. When your dog goes into heat, this information is announced to all eligible males in the vicinity at large by a telltale odor emitted by her urine. Usually before you are even suspicious of this event, the appearance of males at your doorstep will herald its arrival. All too often these ever-anxious suitors will camp themselves around your premises creating a nuisance for you and most probably for your neighbors as well. Action is required before you alienate your entire neighborhood. Either have your dog put into a kennel until the end of her cycle or use special measures such as taking her far from the house to urinate and using a no-odor medication. If you keep your bitch at home, take extreme precautions to protect her from any indiscriminate alliance. Cleanliness is also vital at this time. If she is unable to keep the vulvar area clean, then you must wash this area with warm water.

Care of the Male

The male presents other considerations to his master. Instinctively, most males like to roam— either in search of a female or a companion or just for fun. Those dog owners who live in an area where this is permissible and does not annoy others, are most fortunate. Most dog owners though cannot allow their pets a free reign either because of the danger to the dog himself, or because of the nuisance such freedom causes to the community as reflected in local legal ordinances. A dog running loose is in danger of being hit by a car, of ingesting something poisonous, and even of becoming lost or stolen. All people hate having a neighbor's dog wander onto their property, making deposits which burn their grass, bushes, and soiling and ripping up chunks of their lawn. Thus, out of consideration for others no dog should be allowed to roam. Unfortunately many dog owners are far from considerate which has resulted in "leash laws" being enacted in many communities around the country. These laws prohibit the dog's uninhibited wanderings and enforce this regulation with fines levied against the owner.

The male dog can also become a sex offender by masturbating on furniture and people's legs. So far, there seems to be no real cure for stopping such offensive behavior. Firm correction of this misbehavior seems to be the only remedy although it is far from effective.

A bitch must be protected while in heat, otherwise the result can be an undesired litter of puppies.

Most males like to roam, unfortunately many communities can not tolerate this. (Photo courtesy of American Field.)

Photo by Jane Jacobson

Many communities have leash laws, so if your dog is out "visiting" a fine can result!

Mental Health

Believe it or not, dogs too can have mental health problems. Thus, the best thing to do is try and raise a normal healthy puppy into a well-adjusted dog. This can best be accomplished by providing a happy, relaxed, home environment. The effects of early experiences should not be underestimated. Frightening experiences can do permanent damage to a dog's mode of behavior and personality development. For example, allowing a pup to be mistreated by a child can have the unfortunate consequence of creating a dog who is fearful of children. Fear biters are a menace and are usually too dangerous to keep. *A puppy should never be harshly or cruelly handled.* A calm tension-free environment is best for raising dogs that are not high strung and nervous. Only with love and patience can you expect to create an adult dog that is affectionate and well-tempered.

There are instances when even with the best of environment and care a dog develops unacceptable behavior patterns which do not yield to any form of correction or training. Should you encounter such a difficult animal—one that bites, or attacks and menaces, or one that barks uncontrollably—and you have exhausted all your methods, then by all means seek the services of a professional trainer for remedy. If in spite of professional attention, these traits cannot be eliminated, then seriously consider disposing of the dog. Don't hang on to a potentially hazardous animal until damage has occurred. However, only if the animal is dangerous should it be destroyed. If it has behavior that is unacceptable in your area, remember, it may be tolerated elsewhere. Be honest when disposing of it so that an unfortunate situation isn't perpetuated.

The nature-nurture controversy exists in dogdom just as in humans. One may well question how much a dog's personality is affected by nature (its genetic make-up) and by nurture (its upbringing). Presently, scientists are studying this dilemma. Studies indicate that both aspects play a significant part. Breeding for good temperament is essential and possible. Repeatedly, studies show that nervous, high-strung bitches have a high percentage of nervous, high-strung pups. Well-tempered, calm bitches have a high percentage of pups with these traits. It, therefore, behooves the breeder to be mindful of their bitches' and studs' personality and not to breed those dogs that display personality problems.

Breeding for good temperament is essential. (Photo courtesy of American Field.)

EXERCISE

IN order to keep your dog happy and healthy, a regular daily exercise period is essential. Hunting and working dogs normally receive this vital exercise as a natural part of their existence, however, the house pet is all too often neglected in this area of care. A good brisk walk in the fresh air at least once a day is a minimum standard. Ideally, a one-hour walk is good for keeping the body toned, appetite stimulated, and weight down. Two half-hour walks are also suitable. Unfortunately, there are occasions when neither time nor weather will permit this type of activity. So, some substitutions should be made— a vigorous game of catch, a brief romp in the snow, etc.

The activity must be suitable to the weather since dogs cannot tolerate extremes of temperature. Excess heat can result in heat prostration and undue cold may lead to frostbite. Never leave your dog confined in a car on a hot day because many dogs die needlessly when they are thoughtlessly left in a parked car. The sun beats down on the roof creating a stifling situation and with no escape possible, heat prostration and death can occur rapidly. On a hot day, a dog is best off left at home with adequate ventilation or outside if there is shade and water available. If your dog lives outdoors in a dog house, make certain that it is so situated that it is protected by shade.

Only those animals born and bred for extremely cold weather and outdoor living can be left outside on sub-zero days. Large, heavy-coated dogs prefer living outside in their own house, but even these breeds must have protection during very inclement conditions. All other dogs cannot tolerate extreme

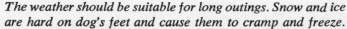

The weather should be suitable for long outings. Snow and ice are hard on dog's feet and cause them to cramp and freeze.

cold and should only be allowed out to relieve themselves. Ideally, an outdoor living setup should provide a means to protect the dog from rain, sun, cold, or danger from theft and injury.

Dogs allowed to exercise independently should have a fenced area such as a yard or dog run of adequate dimensions. If this isn't feasible, a long, nontangle chain device should be used. These special chains can be purchased at pet stores or even made by the "do it yourselfer."

It is generally agreed that any dog of value, be it either monetary or personal, should not be left outside even in a fenced enclosure without any type of supervision available. Our society today contains many "sick" individuals who have been known to maliciously harm unprotected animals or to steal them for monetary gain. Don't invite trouble, always insure your dog's safety by taking all necessary precautions.

How often should a dog be taken out for the purpose of elimination? During puppyhood, even after being housebroken, the pup is not physiologically able to concentrate its urine and will therefore need to go out more frequently than the adult animal. Once a dog is mature enough to concentrate its urine it will have to go out only about three times each day. It is certainly most convenient and pleasurable for our canine friend to be able to come and go at will. Since this is not always possible, training is necessary. Have regular times for these bodily functions and within the short period of a few weeks your dog will have adjusted to this routine. Once in the morning, during the afternoon, and before bed

WALKING YOUR DOG: SENSE AND NONSENSE

How often have you heard someone say that dogs need lots of exercise, or that the city is no place for a dog because dogs need lots of space to roam in, or that a dog needs to wander wherever he wishes in order to be happy?

Good sense? Sheer nonsense! Dogs don't need a lot of exercise. They don't need to be outdoors all day, nor do they want to be. Your dog likes to be with you. If you want to walk, your dog will go along joyously. But if you prefer to sit and read, your dog will be happy to lie beside you.

Dogs who roam the neighborhood usually do so because they are ignored by their owners. They get bored and form the habit of roaming about. And once the habit is formed, it is hard to break. So don't let your dog begin.

make a good minimum schedule. There is usually no reason why your dog should disturb you at an unreasonable early morning hour. Poor training is often the cause for such an irritating habit. Naturally, illness, certain medication, a change in diet, the female's "heat" period, and other such logical reasons can change even the best habits; thus, flexibility is essential.

Exercising these dogs can be a full-time job.

REGULAR GROOMING

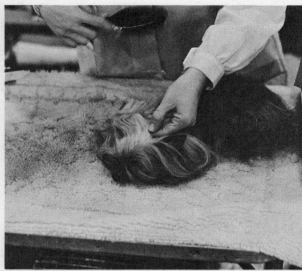

A Yorkshire Terrier requires a great deal of grooming. (Kajimonor Sissy Seymour owned by D. Creeden, Glen Ellyn, Illinois.)

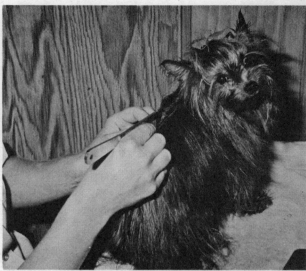

Correct combing involves parting the hair and combing a small section at a time working all the way down to the skin.

GROOMING can be one of the pleasurable experiences you can enjoy with your pet or it can be a trial for you both. Make it a joy from earliest puppyhood and it will be an activity bringing you both great satisfaction. Training your dog to co-operate during the grooming process is the first step. Insist that the young pup lies or stands still while you perform your combing and brushing rites. Speaking softly while tending to his coat will do much to reassure him. Praise him for his good behavior and he will try to please you at each subsequent session. Teach him exactly how you want him to turn and how you wish his head held. Placing him on a table will help make the job easier for you and will encourage his correct attitude. Ideally your dog should learn to jump up on the "grooming" table at your request and to stand as you desire until dismissed. Of course, not all dog owners reach this degree of training, but it's a goal for which to aim. A specially constructed grooming table, such as those used in dog grooming salons, is not necessary. Any table which can be covered with paper and which places the dog at a height comfortable for you is quite adequate. We have even used the top of our washing machine successfully for this job. A large dog may need only a crate, or, if there is nothing else avail-

A steel comb is best for this type of work. Long-haired breeds such as this do best with a daily combing and brushing.

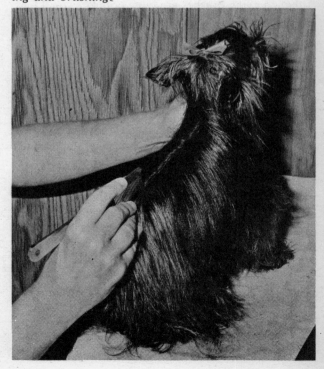

Left—Under all that hair is a Standard Poodle.

Below and right—These dogs are easy to groom because of their smooth coats.

able, there is always the floor. Regular grooming is the important thing—not the equipment.

Equipment

One only needs a few items for the regular, routine grooming which is so essential for your dog's appearance and health. A brush with a good sturdy handle and firm, but not hard, bristles is essential. Although nylon brushes are quite popular, you'll find that a genuine bristle brush lasts longer and seems to do a better job. Such a brush need not necessarily be purchased in the pet department—a "human" one will serve the purpose.

A metal comb is most helpful and you will find a large selection from which to choose. A wide toothed one is used for working out mats and tangles, and the fine toothed one gives that nice finished appearance. One comb having both large and small teeth may be satisfactory for your requirements. In addition to the basic comb and brush, there are other articles you may need or you may think you need. Before buying numerous—possibly unnecessary—items, determine what you actually need. Ask about this when you purchase your dog; ask your

---

Start Grooming Early

Dogs taught to stand for grooming, toe nail clipping, eye cleaning, burr removal, and similar things, while young, learn at that time that they cannot growl at or bite the person working on them.

vet or your local professional dog groomer. If you are doing "special" grooming for a show or if you are doing clipping, then you will need additional equipment.

Short-Haired vs Long-Haired

Smooth-coated or short-haired dogs are the easiest to groom and require the least amount of time. A thorough brushing once a week will keep the coat clean and shiny. Take care not to scrape the skin when combing a smooth-haired dog. Those dogs having long hair or undercoats require more attention. They must be combed with a wide toothed comb and then brushed thoroughly. This procedure will undo mats and tangles as well as removing dead hair, dirt, and stimulating new growth. Correct combing is done by parting the hair and combing a small section at a time working all the way down to the skin. Stroking first in one direction and then in the other makes it possible to get at all of the hairs. Since regular combing and brushing removes dead hairs, you will have less shed hair on your floors and carpets. The really long-haired breeds should be groomed daily to prevent any difficult mats and tangles from forming. A little neglect can have disastrous consequences for when mats are too thick to be coaxed out with a comb, then they must be cut out. As you can well imagine such cutting can result in an unsightly hole in the dog's coat. On occasion, even the frequently groomed pooch can develop a serious tangle which must be cut. Try to work it out

to the smallest possible area and then cut as little as necessary.

Novice dog owners are frequently surprised how much appearance affects their dog. A freshly groomed pet practically struts around like a proud peacock while a neglected or temporarily unsightly hound will slink around and hide whenever possible.

As part of their regular grooming care, some breeds require a little trimming here and there. Hair growing around the anus should be kept short so that excretia doesn't become lodged in it. You may want to trim hair which grows into the eyes and hinders clear vision. Use a blunt round-tipped scissors to prevent accidental injury. Uneven and long hair around the edge of the ear should be cut off neatly in most breeds.

Bathing

Generally, a dog should be bathed only when necessary. Frequent combing and brushing should keep him quite clean and the bath should be reserved for special occasions. When Rover rolls in the mud, or even worse, and the smell is enough to stop anyone at ten paces, then the time has come. Why not bathe more frequently — what harm can it do? Plenty! The typical dog will suffer from dry skin and hair if bathed too often. The natural oils are removed and the coat will lose its shine and luster. Dogs washed too frequently will display a thin soft coat. Unnecessary bathing also needlessly exposes the dog to possible chilling, and eye or ear irritations.

The Bath: Before the bath your dog should be completely brushed and combed since bathing will increase any mats and tangles which exist. The actual mechanics of the bath are quite simple. Have all your necessary equipment and bathing materials at hand before you start since you want to proceed quickly to avoid chilling the dog. Using a laundry tub is ideal because pup won't jump out. Protect the ears and eyes and then wet down the dog thoroughly. The water temperature should be lukewarm, like you would use to bathe a baby. Apply a rich lanolin or protein dog shampoo and rub vigorously through the fur to work up a lather. If there are problems such as dandruff or external parasites, then you will need to use a special shampoo. Several complete and thorough rinses are of utmost importance. A hose with a spray attachment simplifies the procedure. Rinsing is of utmost importance as shampoo remaining on the coat may irritate the skin and will dull the fur. Be certain that the feet are washed and rinsed carefully.

Now comes the drying. With a long-haired dog you should pat off the excess moisture, others can just be towel dried. Vigorous rubbing with several turkish towels should get your soppy friend damp dry. If he will then submit to being dried by an electric hair dryer, your job is much easier. Many dogs are deathly afraid of a dryer though and it isn't worth creating a problem. Continue drying until your dog feels practically dry. Pay special attention to the ears to be certain that they are completely dry. Wipe them clean with cotton dipped in a little oil.

Now you may brush and comb your clean and fresh smelling companion. If his coat has a tendency to be unusually dry and brittle, you may wish to use a special spray for this condition. Or if your purpose in bathing the dog was to combat external parasites, then apply whatever powder was prescribed as treatment. While you are drying and grooming during this clean stage you can most easily observe your dog's skin. Check it for any problems; investigate those areas that he's been scratching. This is too good an opportunity to miss.

It's generally advised to keep the dog in for at least six to 12 hours after a bath if the weather is cool or wet.

The Nails

A dog's nails should be kept cut quite short to keep his feet feeling comfortable and neat in appearance. Walking on long nails will spread the toes, thus adversely affecting the dog's gait, as well as presenting the danger of their being caught and torn accidentally which can cause great pain.

Cutting the nails regularly is recommended. Special pet nail cutting scissors are available for this purpose. Proceed with this task most cautiously as the quick above nail bed is highly sensitive and will bleed and cause extreme pain if cut. Once a dog has been hurt he will usually resent having his nails cut. Some dogs are so terrified of have their nails touched, often because of some previous injury, that only a vet or professional can handle them.

In white nailed dogs, the quick, which is pink, is visible and cutting too short can be avoided. However, black nails are difficult to judge and the novice should not attempt it. Using a file may be preferable at first until you learn to gauge correctly. Frequent cutting helps the quick to recede. The section to cut is the hook which curves downward.

City dogs that walk on sidewalks a great deal keep their nails filed down and need cutting infrequently. By filing the nails with a regular canine file, they can be kept shortened without frequent cutting.

The Teeth

Tartar deposits may form on your dog's teeth if his diet contains inadequate amounts of hard biscuits or rawhide bones. These black tartar deposits should be removed since they cause recession and irritation of the gums. Have your veterinarian show you how this is done and then you can handle this chore should deposits continue to form. If you wish, you can brush his teeth with baking soda, salt, or a mild pumice. The best care though is providing chewable material which will clean the teeth.

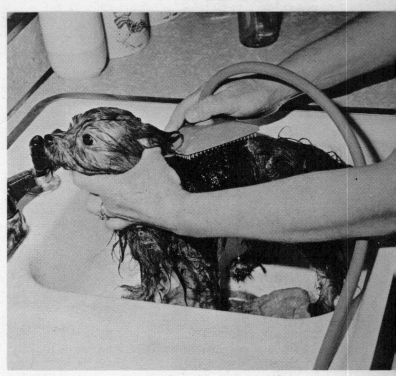

A small dog can be washed in the sink and a spray simplifies the procedure.

Rinsing thoroughly is essential. A long haired dog may require eight to ten minutes of rinsing.

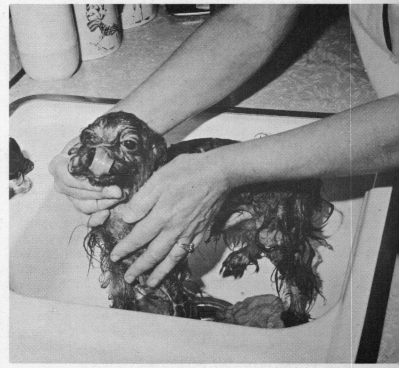

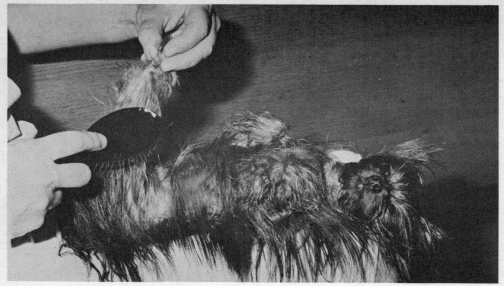

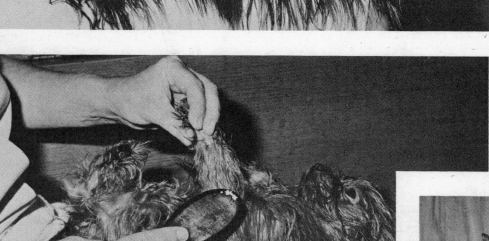

Left—After the bath and the drying it is brush, brush, brush —layer by layer. Center—The coat is brushed in the opposite direction of its natural fall and then brushed back when the dog is in the standing position. Below left—Cut the dog's nails carefully, you may find that placing the dog on his back simplifies the procedure. Below right—What an ordeal! But, once it's over the result is a pleasure to behold.

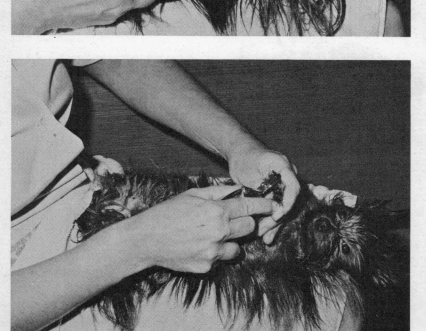

TRAINING

HOUSEBREAKING

MANY puppies start their housebreaking training while they are still with their mother in the whelping box. Since dogs instinctively like to sleep in a clean area, they will usually relieve themselves away from where they want to lie. By having newspaper covering most of the whelping box floor, they begin to identify the paper as a good place to "go." With this background already in existence, the new owner has a good start with paper training.

Three months of age is when housebreaking is started, and the kitchen is a fine spot. Here, the pup is apt to have lots of company, and it is a location which normally has a washable floor covering and makes confinement possible. Spread several layers of newspaper over most of the floor and barricade the puppy so that he is confined to this area. Puppy's bed, food dish, and water pan should also be in this spot. The little pup will generally select one corner in which to relieve himself. Praise him, and reduce the size of the paper covered area. Always remove the soiled newspaper, but leave a sheet on

Puppy Training Tip

Some pups can be house-broken in a day; some not for long weeks. (Even as some children can learn to read in a day, while others take an interminable time over the task.) In house-breaking, more than in anything and everything else in his training, patience and common sense—especially the latter—must come into action.

top which still has the special odor. The odor will tell him that this is the spot, and he will use it again.

Praise and patience are the key ingredients in housebreaking a puppy. When he relieves himself on the newspaper, praise him lavishly. If he makes a mistake, scold him gently, pick him up, and put him on the paper. Remember, this must be done at the time of the "accident," not later. During this period, it is so important for someone to be able to devote a great deal of time to training. Unless you are present and able to indicate to the puppy exactly what you expect, learning will be very slow.

Allow nature to help you in this housebreaking procedure. Puppies relieve themselves immediately on waking in the morning and when awakening from naps, as well as after meals. Place the puppy on the paper at these times and you will be nicely rewarded.

During these first few weeks of serious paper training, restrict your punishment to a stern "No" and a shake of the finger. Show the dog what you expect rather than punishing him for his errors. Don't slap him, hit him with a newspaper, or stick his nose in his mistake. Since he is only a baby, these methods are much too severe.

By the age of four months, you can begin the real outdoor housebreaking. Transfer the paper to where you want him to go. Observe the puppy closely and when he heads to where the paper was located previously, pick him up and carry him outside to the new location. Continue to anticipate and

When housebreaking one puppy or an entire litter remember to keep your instructions simple and to always use the same terms. Until fully house-broken a dog should not be given the run of the house. (Crown Jewel Puppies.)

take the pup out first thing in the morning, after eating, at noon, after nap, and before going to bed for the night. Until housebreaking is really going quite successfully, continue to keep the pup confined. If he is given the run of the house, accidents are bound to happen. Once he really has the message, try to develop a good schedule. Remember, a young dog is not physically able to hold his urine for a long span of time. The schedule will probably be at least six times a day. Mistakes will occur, correct them immediately — take him to the place he made the error, show it to him, and then lead him outside. Keep your instructions simple and always use the same terms.

Until the puppy is well housebroken and old enough to control himself, put newspapers down whenever you must leave the house. This way your baby can be "good" and you won't have to clean up any accidents and do any scolding.

Some breeds train very easily and others are more difficult. Don't get discouraged if you find training isn't progressing as rapidly as you expected, and don't allow bad habits to develop. Firmness and consistency will pay off at the end. *Until the dog is fully trained, don't give him the run of the house.* If a relapse occurs after training, confine him again until he can be trusted. Since housebreaking is really one of the most important lessons to be learned, insist on complete compliance before you relax. There is nothing more annoying than a dog that cannot be trusted in the house.

Think twice about trying to housebreak a puppy of one of the large breeds. When they have an accident, it is quite a mess. Professionals recommend that you have it trained elsewhere, and bring it home after it is able to function on a four times a day exercise schedule.

REVIEW OF HOUSEBREAKING

- Enclose the dog in a small area. The kitchen is good.
- Begin by paper training.
- Use praise. Be patient. Correct mistakes immediately.
- When paper is mastered transfer outdoors.
- Keep at it until 100 per cent consistency is attained.

YARDBREAKING

While you are housebreaking your dog, you ought also to yard break him. You are already taking him to the same spot which may be behind or beside the garage. You can—and should—teach him not to use other sections of your yard.

Some fully trained dogs will leave a puddle to show resentment.

Special Problems

Believe it or not, some fully trained dogs seem to use anti-housebreaking behavior to display their anger or resentment. They will leave a puddle or deposit to show their disappointment when left home alone or in response to some punishment. Needless to say, such behavior cannot be tolerated, and a firm stand must be taken.

Training and Consideration

Now a special word about a special problem— where to exercise your dog. It is amazing how many dog owners are apparently oblivious to the resentment that they create in their neighbors by allowing their dogs to use the neighbor's property as a bathroom. In fact, some dog owners will actually walk their dog over to a neighbor's rather than allow him to use their own lawn. This type of behavior is definitely anti-social and most obnoxious. Dog owners should have more sense and consideration. By all means, give your dog a walk. However, don't allow him to make a mess on other people's lawns, walks, or gardens. Keep him on a lead and take him to an empty lot to relieve himself. City dogs must be curb trained—that is trained to make in the roadway. If you have a yard, the dog can be taught to use a special section for this purpose, and you can clean it up regularly. Should your dog make a mistake and use the neighbor's lawn, scold him and train him *not* to repeat this act. Your pet should not become a nuisance to anyone else.

SPECIAL TRAINING

MOST pet owners get great satisfaction from having their dogs display ability in doing some tricks.

BEGGING — OR — "SIT UP"

The young puppy often begs instinctively when some tidbit is held up in front of him. Should "junior" try to jump for the morsel, just scold him gently and push him back down. Begging can be learned rapidly so just repeat this exercise several times, giving a reward for the correct response and you'll have a little pup with one trick mastered.

SPEAKING

Having a dog that will bark on command is not only fun, but it can also be helpful at times. The easiest way to teach this trick is to initially say "Speak" when the dog barks voluntarily in order to help him associate the word with the act. Then, offer him a treat and command him to "Speak." When he finally barks, reward him with much praise and the treat. Repeat this lesson until he readily gives a loud bark when given the command.

"FETCH"

There are many other tricks that a dog can be taught, such as shaking hands, rolling over, jumping through a hoop, playing dead, and fetching. Undoubtedly, fetching is the most important as it can become part of a regular training program for advanced obedience or for field work, or it can be just for fun so that the dog can participate in a game of catch. Puppyhood is an ideal time to teach this trick since these youngsters love to put everything in their mouth. Tempt Rover with a ball or dumbbell or toy, then throw it and shout "Fetch." When the pup retrieves the object, he may stop and play and chew it. Encourage him to return directly to you and to give the ball back. A long lead will be helpful when training for this trick. Having fun, giving praise, and repetition will speed learning. You'll find this trick will give you, your family, and your dog a great deal of enjoyment.

"SHAKE HANDS"

A dog should be taught not to jump on people. Shaking hands is a more pleasant way for him to greet guests. It's an easy trick to teach. Put your dog in a normal sitting position and kneel in front of him. Tap the back of his foreleg with your hand. When he lifts his paw, take it gently in your hand and say "Shake" or "Shake hands." Smile and tell him he's a good dog.

"JUMP"

Jumping is fun for a long-legged dog and good exercise, too. Build a low bar—a long straight stick

Teaching your dog to "Fetch" can lead to bigger and better things, such as retrieving.

A GENERAL TRAINING RULE!

YOUR DOG MUST ALWAYS THINK HE IS A SUCCESS—this is the *sine qua non* of dog training. According to research, lack of success is the most common reason why some dogs fail to learn. Even if your dog gives a seemingly inadequate performance, it is essential that he feels he has done something right —something to merit your praise. Your praise is what he wants more than anything else.

When your dog has difficulty learning a new lesson, go back and repeat one that he has already mastered. Then you can honestly praise his performance, giving his ego a boost. He'll be ready to try the new lesson again.

Tone of voice is one of the keys to successful dog training. In fact, some professional trainers name it as the most important factor in training.

Do dogs understand words? Animal behavior experts have differing opinions, comments the Gaines Dog Research Center. Some behaviorists hold that dogs do not comprehend the actual meaning of words. Others believe the average dog has a 30-50 word vocabulary; exceptional animals, up to 1,000-word vocabulary.

However, the experts generally agree it's not what you say that counts, but how you say it.

Do you react favorably to a shrill nagging voice? No? Neither does your dog. You're much more inclined to respond to a pleasant tone and so is the dog.

Training commands should be delivered in a well-modulated voice that's warm but decisive.

Of course the basic tone changes with the situation. The "come" command, for example, lends itself to an eager voice, encouraging the dog to come quickly and directly to you.

On the other hand, a reprimand, "no!" or "bad dog!" needs a firm, disapproving tone. Effectively delivered, it's often scolding enough without being reinforced with a slap or shaking.

No command should be given in hesitant or unsure tones. The dog senses your lack of conviction. This tone of voice doesn't urge obedience. Instead, it invites a let's-see-what-can-be-gotten-away-with reaction.

Nor should commands be shouted unless the dog is outdoors and not within normal hearing range. Shouting is not necessary under ordinary circumstances. Don't forget the dog's hearing is acute. A loud voice is painful to him and won't make him more clearly understand your wishes.

Raising your voice in anger also is poor training procedure. You may frighten the dog into obeying but probably only will frighten him, period, and confuse him.

Know what you want the dog to do and tell him. Use a tone of voice that makes the command clear, and encourges his cheerful, obedient response.

or broom handle laid across two or three piled up bricks. Put a training collar and lead on your dog. Walk him quickly toward the bar. When you want him to jump, give a quick, upward jerk on the collar and say "Jump." Practice this trick with the stick raised higher and higher until he can jump twice his shoulder height.

Training the Biter

It is not unusual for a dog to snap or bite if you try to take something away which he has and wants. Training to avoid this form of behavior is essential. When the dog refuses to surrender what he has, don't grab it! Firmly command "Drop it" or "Give me," and, if he lets go of the object, praise him. When it's something that he can have, return it. If he won't surrender his booty, quickly and quietly without growling, then follow one of these techniques:

1—**If he is a small dog, pick him up by the collar, and hold him until he releases the bone or whatever.**
2—**With a larger dog, slap him across the rump with a rolled up newspaper.**
3—**Or, slap him across the nose with a rolled up paper.**

Never put your hand out to take something if the dog growls menacingly at you. Be firm and speak strictly until the item is dropped. Even the best pet has been known to bite his master's hand if he tries to remove a favorite bone.

Need Extra Help?

If you know that you don't have the time, patience or know-how to train your dog alone you may wish to have a dog training school assist you. Now there are schools which provide trainers who come to the home and teach you and your dog together. The typical pet may have a "home" course in house breaking and responding to basic obedience commands. This type of course usually runs from five to seven weeks and the tuition costs from $150 to $250. More advanced or specialized training such as protection or conformation will cost much more.

Be sure you deal with a reputable firm that has well trained instructors and that provides some guarantee of success.

Conclusion

Training and education is *not* a once in a lifetime event. Puppies and young dogs are not the only ones that can profit from this type of attention. All dogs need to have their training refreshed and their education expanded. It isn't true that you can't teach an old dog new tricks—you can.

DOG TRAINING TIPS

THE DOG training tips presented here outline the exact methods which the average dog owner can use to teach his dog the five basic obedience commands which every housedog should know and obey.

Diligent application of these step-by-step instructions will result not only in a well-trained dog, but also in a happier, more satisfying relationship between dog and master.

This material was compiled by Pet Food Institute with the assistance of Willy Necker, famous trainer of thousands of dogs. Mr. Necker was head of War Dog Training for the U.S. Coast Guard during World War II, and also trained many U.S. Army men and dogs.

GENERAL TRAINING SUGGESTIONS

1—Conduct short, business-like training sessions, twice a day, if possible.

2—Give the dog exercise before each lesson begins, with ample opportunity to relieve himself.

3—Begin each lesson with a review of one or more previous lessons so that the dog can earn praise right from the start, putting you both in a good mood.

4—Make all commands definite and clear. Be firm.

5—Never let yourself become impatient with your dog. One quality you must exercise is patience.

6—Never let your dog disregard even one of your commands. From the first lesson on, once you give an order, see that it is obeyed. Stick with it. If you let a dog disobey you once, ignore one single command, he will feel that he can do it again. Your goal is to see that your dog never even suspects that he can do anything other than mind you. Your command must be law to him.

7—Always end each lesson with some improvement. If you are working on one of harder subjects, you may ease up a little if necessary in order to let the dog be successful. The dog must always succeed; if he fails to merit praise, keep on with it until he does accomplish his goal, even though slowly and clumsily. Quitting on a note of success, and meriting profuse praise, does wonders for the dog's morale.

8—If at all possible, conduct the lessons in strict privacy, without distractions. You should be able to obtain the dog's complete attention.

9—If any particular lesson is not going well, and relations between you and your pupil are becoming a bit strained, it is a good idea to switch to a review lesson for a few minutes to give you an excuse to praise and pet the dog, before resuming the tougher task. You will both feel a lot better for the interlude.

HEEL

When a dog is commanded to HEEL, he walks without force or urging, at his handler's side with his right shoulder about even with the handler's left knee. If on leash, the leash hangs loose. If off leash, the dog walks equally well in the same position.

How to hold the leash: Snap the short leash on the collar with your dog at your left, pass the leash through a circle formed by your thumb and first and second fingers of your left hand. The end of the leash is held in your right hand. Hold your left hand and arm at your side in your usual walking position. Your dog can walk comfortably with a slack leash, and you can easily check him quickly if you hold him in this manner. Get the dog on your left side, give the command "HEEL" and walk forward. For the first lesson, don't pay much attention to the manner in which he goes —it is enough that he goes with you. Use the word "HEEL" often. During succeeding lessons keep him fairly well in the correct position. When he gets ahead of you, bring him back, commanding "HEEL" and at the same time make him mind by giving him quick, sharp jerks on the leash. DO NOT BRING HIM TO YOU BY SUSTAINED PULLING ON THE LEASH. Give him a little slack in the leash when he is heeling as he should. Then, if he drops behind or forges ahead, correct him with the vocal command and jerking on the leash. Keep at this, lesson after lesson, until your dog heels in the correct position without tugging at the leash. The dog must adapt himself to your changes of pace and direction. When you step backward or sideward, walk fast or slow, the dog must instantly do the same. As you make right or left turns, your dog must maintain his position at your left side, speeding his gait when you turn to the right or slowing it when you make a left turn. When you turn to walk in the opposite direction, it will make it easier for the dog to understand if you will hesitate a moment or step backward one step before reversing your direction.

DOWN

When a dog is commanded DOWN, he must immediately drop to a lying position. He must do this whether, at the moment of command, he is heeling, sitting, standing, running or walking.

Have the dog SIT at your left side. Drop to your left knee. With your left hand gripping the leash close to his collar, give it short, sharp jerks downward. Say "DOWN" "DOWN" "DOWN." Repeat this procedure again and again.

Some dogs will fight this lesson, and the trainer must persevere, with a great many repetitions. If your dog is stubborn, refusing to go down, use your right hand to pull his forefeet out from under him while giving him the verbal command and jerking downwards on the leash.

It helps to give the verbal command repeatedly, even during the time the dog actually is DOWN! He can't hear it too often while he is learning.

With this command, as well as with the command SIT, unless you order him to STAY, he must instantly get up and HEEL when you start to walk away.

This exercise has a depressing effect on most dogs, so it is well not to keep at it very long at a time. Be sure to give your pet plenty of praise and encouragement when he does a good job of it—not, however, when he is in the DOWN position. Then he should not be petted by anyone. If you do, he'll want to get right back up.

In teaching this command, vary your routine and don't always give various commands in the same order. As soon as he knows DOWN, give him the command at times other than when he is heeling. You want this command to be obeyed instantly no matter where the dog is or what he is doing.

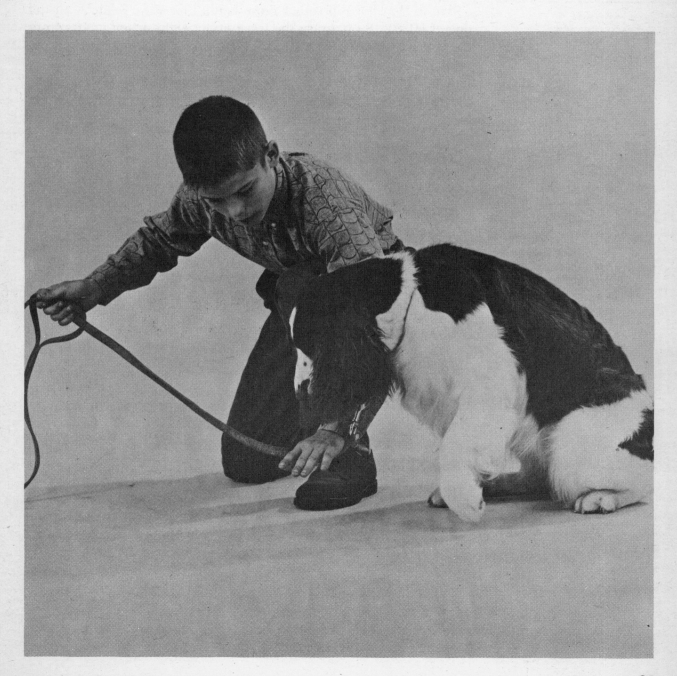

SIT

When commanded to SIT, the dog must promptly assume the sitting posture, squarely on both hips. He must SIT at once, whether, at the moment of command, he is heeling, running or lying down.

Put the dog's choke collar and short leash on him. Arrange the collar so that it is up rather close behind his ears. Walk with the dog at HEEL. Stop, grasp the leash about eight or ten inches from the collar with your right hand. Order "SIT." Jerk upward sharply on the leash and press down with your left hand on his hind quarters. All of this action takes place simultaneously: the command, the upward jerk on the leash, the downward push on the dog's back. Keep repeating the command, "SIT."

Resume your walk, telling the dog to HEEL as you start out. Take a few steps and repeat the whole performance. Keep this up for about 15 minutes, long enough for the first few lessons.

While he is learning what is meant by the word SIT, you need not be very much concerned about how he sits. After he knows and obeys the command, however, you should always have him SIT in the proper position—facing in the same direction as his handler, his head even with or slightly ahead of his handler's knees and with about six inches separating them.

To teach him to SIT in the proper position, help him each time it is necessary. As he assumes the sitting posture, swing his rear to the correct spot as he is going down. Use your left hand for this, holding his leash near the collar with your right. If he tries to SIT too far ahead of you or behind you, jerk him with the leash to the correct spot.

When he has mastered this routine, he must assume the sitting position promptly whenever you give the command, whether he is walking or lying down. When the handler resumes his walk, the dog must, without further command, get up and resume heeling unless he has been commanded to stay.

As soon as he will obey this command without help, the same routine must be run through with a loose leash. When perfect results are obtained on a loose leash, the pupil graduates to working this command off leash entirely.

STAY

The command STAY may be given while the dog is standing, sitting or lying down. At the command he should remain in the position he held when it was given.

Put your dog on his short leash. Command him to go DOWN. Tell him to STAY. Walk around him, keeping the end of the leash in hand, but do not tighten up on it. When he starts to get up, say "No, STAY." Back away from him; go sideways from him; step over him. Each time he starts to get up, repeat "No, STAY." Each time he tries to follow you when you walk away from him, you must command him to go DOWN again·

Soon he will STAY while you walk to the end of the short leash, while you walk around him, or even while you jump over him. You will have to try all of these if you want to make a good "stayer" out of him.

After he has made considerable progress, vary the routine by having him SIT while you repeat the procedure. When you feel that he is proficient when worked on the short leash, start work with the long one. Put the dog DOWN at your side. Wad up the surplus length of leash in your hand and throw it out away from you. Command him to STAY, repeating the word several times. Turn and walk to the free end of the leash. If he rises, rush right back and make him go DOWN again. Repeat the command STAY and walk away once more. Your immediate objective is to be able to walk to the end of the long leash, pick it up, turn and face the dog for a few minutes, while he remains quietly in position until you call him to you. Work on this until he will STAY in this way.

To have him STAY while you are completely out of sight, pick a quiet room and put the dog DOWN. Order him to STAY and leave the room. Watch him, if possible, through a crack in the door and, if he shows signs of getting up, go to him and repeat the command. Don't hesitate to use the word STAY again and again.

At first, leave him for only about one minute. Then, as he improves, gradually increase the time you stay away to around ten minutes. Each time that you come back and find that he has obeyed your order, have him SIT and then praise and pet him. (Praise the dog for good work in obeying the STAY command only after he has been released from it.)

To continue these lessons, take him out of doors, put him on his long leash and fasten this to a tree or post, restraining him from wandering away. Tell him to STAY, then go out of his sight and find a spot where you can observe his actions. Repeat the same procedure you used indoors. Take care that he does not chew the leash or otherwise misbehave while he is alone. If he does, it calls for a very sharp reprimand.

This exercise, making your dog obey you even though you are apparently not around to enforce your will upon him, is very important. The effect it has on the dog is to make him more obedient to all commands. He will get to feel that you know everything he does and that he must obey every order.

COME

When the dog is called, he must immediately COME to you, running or trotting, and when he reaches you he must SIT in front of and facing you, awaiting your further orders.

Have the dog on his long leash. Command him to DOWN, STAY. Toss the free end of the leash away, walk over to the end, pick it up, turn around and face your dog. Call him to you. Use his name in connection with the command "Duke, COME." The tone of your voice should be serious, commanding, not coaxing or wheedling. If he doesn't COME, reel him in hand over hand. Practice the lesson until he begins to obey and shows that he understands the words. Then you can change the routine a little. Leave the long leash stretched along the ground but not actually attached to his collar. Call him as before. If he is slightly hesitant, go so far as to pull in the leash. Even though it isn't attached to the dog he will think it is.

Next step is to work without using the leash at all. If he continues to COME the moment he is called, continue to work him off-leash. If, however, he ignores the command, get the leash out again for a little concentrated review.

When your dog reaches you, have him SIT in front of you for a few seconds before you pet him. This obviates any tendency he might develop to jump on you. If he does not SIT directly in front of you or close enough, seize the leash close to his collar and back away from him repeating the command, "COME, COME." After he has been sitting properly for a few seconds, command him to HEEL. Then you are free to, and should, praise and pet him.

Your dog should COME to you without delay, head up, on the double when you call him. If he takes his time, pull and jerk him on the long leash.

Never punish or scold your dog after he has COME to you even though he has not done it the way he should. If you punish him when he arrives in front of you, he will be confused, thinking the punishment was for coming to you, not for the manner in which he came.

FEEDING

A DOG'S DIETARY NEEDS*

SMALL dogs require more food per pound of body weight than large ones. The usual adult house dog weighing 12 to 14 pounds needs approximately one-third of a pound of dry food, 6 oz. of some moist food, or one can of complete dog food per day.

Growing puppies need about twice as many calories as the adult dog.

One generous meal of well-balanced, nourishing complete dog food is sufficient for the normal adult dog. If the owner prefers, there is no harm in feeding twice a day, just as long as the dog is not overfed. Frequent tidbits between meals are apt to reduce the appetite and may develop finicky eating habits.

Any food left at mealtime should be removed and discarded within a reasonable time after the dog loses interest; no other food should be provided until the next regular feeding time. If the dog becomes obese, the volume of food should be reduced even though he may beg for more. Mature spayed or castrated animals, old or very inactive dogs, may retain large appetites, but they require 25 to 50 per cent less food than younger more active dogs.

Ideally, dogs should be fed at the same time each day. Dogs appreciate regularity. Regular feeding often helps maintain steady appetites.

Provision for sufficient water is important. The requirement is self-regulated, depending on such factors as the type of food, environmental temperature, amount of exercise, and the temperament of the dog. The need can be satisfied by permitting the dog free access to water at all times. A dog should not be allowed large amounts of cold water immediately following violent exercise.

A sudden change of diet may upset the digestive system of a dog. If a new type of food is to be fed, it is advisable to make the change gradually by replacing some of the original diet with the new food over a period of a week or more before the latter becomes the total diet. By making a change in foods a gradual process, digestive upsets causing diarrhea or other temporary conditions can be avoided.

Dogs seem to thrive on monotony. Scientific tests indicate that the average dog prefers the food to which he has become accustomed the earliest and longest.

Numerous studies have established that a diet con-

*Excerpts from *Basic Guide to Canine Nutrition*. Gaines Dog Research Center. New York, 1965.

taining a sufficient amount of bulk to induce stool elimination is more beneficial to the dog than one producing hard stools and constipation. This is the reason all well-balanced prepared dog foods supply a small amount of fiber in the ration.

Dog foods represent a unique concept. Unlike foods prepared for human beings, the high quality commercially prepared dog food must be a complete diet. The commercial dog food manufacturer starts with the premise that the dog food being prepared is to be the sole diet of the animal; no other food will be required. Thus, the food plus water represents a complete, well-balanced diet.

COMMERCIAL DOG FOODS

Dry Dog Foods

Meals, either in flakes or pellet-type foods, usually are quite complete nutritionally; the *best* of them *may* be adequate for the lifelong activities of dogs.

Biscuits and Kibbles

Biscuit-type foods are *not* usually fed as a complete diet, even though some brands are nutritionally complete. These foods may be used as snacks or training treats.

Semi-Moist Dog Foods

Nutritionally complete, semi-moist dog food supplies adequate amounts of the essential nutrients for bitches in gestation and lactation, as well as growing puppies, old dogs, and normal adult dogs.

Canned Dog Foods

A complete dog food which is a blend of meat or meat by-products with the addition of cereals, other plant products, vitamins, minerals, and fats can be found in canned dog food.

Canned Meats

Canned meats are *not* considered complete diets but are intended for mixing with complete dog foods for palatability.

Because the dog is classed as a carnivore, many persons assume that his ideal diet should consist solely of meat. *The fact is that a dog fed entirely on meat would soon be undernourished and in poor condition.*

Self Feeding

Self feeding is one of the newer practices that is gaining in popularity. The puppy or adult dog feeds himself from a container in which dry meal is always available. He can eat as much as he wants whenever he wants it. An available supply of fresh water is essential is a self-feeding program.

A dog maintains an even level of nutrients in his bloodstream by eating when he is hungry. A self feeding program minimizes boredom and reduces the damage dogs will do to furniture and rugs. If the owner is away from home during the scheduled feeding time, the dog can satisfy his hunger.

Some puppies or dogs may overeat and become fat on a self-feeding regimen, but most animals will eat the amount needed for appropriate weight gain and growth, particularly if this system is begun as soon as a pup is old enough to chew dry foods easily, rather than long after his feeding habits have become well established.

Partial self feeding is an alternative plan. With this method, puppies are fed one or even two regular feedings a day which are supplemented by self feeding.

Feeding Animals with Specific Diseases

Dogs that have medical problems require special consideration in their nutrition.

KIDNEY DISEASE

Foods given the animal with kidney disease must be nutritious, palatable, and of the highest quality. Proteins in the diet of the dog with kidney disease should consist of high quality commercial canned foods or semi-moist rations to which ground glandular organs of liver, kidney, pancreas, ground muscle meat, cottage cheese, and hard boiled eggs are added. Additional carbohydrates in the form of cooked cereals may also be advantageous. Cooked prepared

Above—A good, well-balanced diet keeps a dog in top condition. Below—Growing puppies require twice as many calories as the adult dog.

42

cereals, such as oatmeal, farina, and boiled rice are energy-laden and helpful. Small amounts of polyunsaturated oils are useful as fat.

During a 24 hour period, it is desirable that these animals be given frequent small meals rather than one or two large meals. The food should be well salted; not only do these patients need sodium, but salt will stimulate water turnover in the body which is desirable.

Commercially prepared diets for the dog with kidney disease are available and can be obtained from your veterinarian.

GASTROINTESTINAL DISEASES

These dogs are not only unable to digest many foods properly, but also are somewhat nutritionally depleted because of vomiting or diarrhea. Foods given animals in this category must be bland, low in fiber, appetizing, nutritious, and well-supplemented with water-soluble vitamins.

Animals with gastrointestinal diseases should be fed small, frequent meals. In addition, only small amounts of water should be given at a time. Of course, the water ration may be given at fairly frequent intervals.

Canned special diets fulfilling the requirements of this category are commercially available to veterinarians. These are very convenient and efficient.

PANCREATIC INSUFFICIENCY

These dogs require very special dietary consideration. In general, the diet should contain minimal amounts of fat, most of the caloric intake being supplied by moderate amounts of carbohydrate and protein. In addition, pancreatic enzymes must be administered as replacement therapy.

DIABETES

Dogs suffering from diabetes require very close supervision of their nutritional needs. A balance must be struck between quantity and character of food ingested, activity that the animal is allowed, and the amount of insulin to be administered.

At the onset, the dog must be hospitalized to establish the proper insulin dosage, as well as the amount of food and energy expenditure.

A Puppy's Schedule

You can avoid almost all house accidents if you'll remember that the times when puppy has to relieve himself are immediately on waking in the morning, when awakening from naps, after meals, and during the excitement of play. If you want to play in the house with your puppy, then take him out to his spot first, and again immediately when he shows signs of losing interest in the game.

OBESITY

Obesity is a common canine disease and represents a serious health hazard.

The reducing diet given to an obese dog should be low in fat, high in protein and moderate in carbohydrate with adequate amounts of vitamins and minerals. It is wise to give two or more feedings per day so that the animal will have minimum hunger problems. A reducing diet consists of less than the dog's normal basal requirements.

"SANITATION PROBLEMS"

A low-residue diet resulting in minimum bowel evacuation is desirable for animals with special problems such as fracture of the pelvis, abscess of the anal sacs and surgery in the anal area.

Foods that are rather completely digested should be used to produce a low-residue evacuation. Ground, glandular, or muscle meat, cottage cheese, boiled eggs and cooked cereals will fulfill the need under these circumstances.

SEVERE CARDIOVASCULAR DISTURBANCES

Dogs suffering from severe cardiovascular disturbances require a diet low in sodium (salt) and moderately high in protein and carbohydrates.

There is a commercially available low-salt dog food.

SKIN PROBLEMS

Nutritional problems will often be manifested by skin lesions. Internal parasites can cause skin problems by interfering with normal absorption of nutrients. Any animal with a skin problem should receive a high level, high quality, protein diet. Moderate amounts of fat in the form of polyunsaturated fats should be available, and carbohydrates in adequate amounts for energy are necessary. In addition, the diet should be very adequate in vitamins and minerals. Possible supplementation of a standard commercial diet is quite effective if the cause of the skin problem is definitely nutritional.

LIVER DISEASE

Fat and protein metabolism are greatly influenced by liver function. For this reason, diet consideration as well as other therapy is very important in these dogs.

The diet fed to an animal with liver disease should contain minimal amounts of fat, only enough protein to replace normal loss and high amounts of carbohydrate, to supply energy requirements. In addition, therapeutic amounts of the B group of vitamins and required doses of the fat soluble group of vitamins should be given.

SPECIAL FEEDING

Feeding the Breeding Bitch

Feeding breeding bitches a well-balanced ration in the correct amount is important. Breeding stock in poor body condition and receiving an inadequate diet during gestation and lactation will have a low-milk supply and small pups.

Brood females can be kept on a maintenance ration between litters. At no time should she be overweight. An overweight female can have whelping problems and produce small litters. During the last two to three weeks of the gestation period, her feed consumption will tend to increase as much as 20 per cent as compared to the amount being consumed during maintenance. Usually if the female is fed on a maintenance level of ½ oz. of food per pound of body weight, her increased weight gain will boost food consumption adequately during gestation.

During lactation a bitch may consume 2½-3 times the normal maintenance level by the time the pups are three to four weeks of age. She should have all she wants to eat for the increased food intake necessary to meet the demands of heavy milk production. Since pups start eating solid food by the time they are three to four weeks of age, their feed consumption will increase while the dam's feed consumption will decrease. The ration the dam receives should also be available to her pups.

On the day of weaning the dam should not be fed but should have water available. The second day feed ¼th the normal maintenance level; on the third day ½; on the fourth day ¾ths; and, on the fifth day the amount of food offered is brought up to the normal maintenance level. Cutting back on her food intake and then gradually increasing it helps decrease milk production and aids in the maintenance of a healthy mammary gland.

Stud dogs should be kept in good body condition without being overweight.

Feeding Orphan Puppies

Quite often the bitch will not nurse her puppies or perhaps has died from whelping complications. Here are some methods of handling the problem of orphan puppies.

Feeding—Good commercial bitch milk replacers, such as Borden's Esbilac, are available but if you find yourself in a bind with none available, the following formula can be used:

    1 Cup Evaporated Milk
    1 Tablespoon Corn Oil
  + Vitamin Drops for children
       (Deca-Vi-Sol mfg. by Mead Johnson)
    1 Cup Water
    1 Egg Yolk (no whites)
    A Pinch of Salt

Warm the formula to body temperature and place in Pyrex baby nursing bottles like those used for feeding premature infants.

When feeding the puppies (every 8 hrs. is enough) hold the bottle so the puppy does not ingest air. Hold puppy's body parallel to the floor with the head slightly elevated. There is a tendency the first time to hold a pup's body vertically; this makes it easy for milk to enter the lungs. If milk flows into the lungs, pneumonia will result.

After each feeding take a piece of cotton dipped in warm oil or a clean, moistened wash cloth to massage the puppy and stimulate defecation and urination. Gentle massage of the back and sides before feeding is a form of passive exercise, stimulating circulation and awakening the puppy. Simple grooming is also best done at feeding time. Incubator conditions tend to dry the coat, so rubbing baby oil into the skin is often desirable. However, grooming can be overdone and the puppies should not be disturbed except at feeding time.

Weaning—Puppies can start eating (at 3 weeks of

age) on solid foods along with the mother's milk or milk replacer. By 6 weeks of age they can be fed entirely on solid foods. During the first several months of the puppy's life, keep food before him at all times.

Feeding Hard-Working Dogs

Working dogs use a lot of energy. To replace this energy a large amount of high quality, nutritious food is required. These dogs should be offered all of the dog food they want, but should not be allowed to become overweight.

Feeding once a day is ample, unless weight is a problem, and the dog is thin. Then twice a day feeding may be necessary. Usually the best time to feed is in the evening and dogs should not be fed just prior to being worked. Feed all of the dog food they will clean up—if fed moistened. If the dogs are self-fed dry, then a constant supply of dry food can be left in front of them at all times. If the dog is not maintaining good condition on dry feeding, then he should be switched to moistened dry dog food, since moistening the ration will increase acceptance and the dogs will eat more.

If a hard-working dog does not stay in good body condition using a regular moistened dry dog food, then it is recommended that up to 20 per cent meat be added. The meat does not affect the nutritional balance of a good dry dog food but in most cases will increase the palatability and thus increase the food intake.

During the time a dog is not working, care should be taken to not overfeed, thus creating a weight problem. The average dog, not working, needs about 62 Calories (kcal.) per pound of body weight per day. This will vary according to age, weight, sex, breed, and previous nutrition.

Bones

Dogs like to chew on bones. But don't give them chicken, turkey, or duck bones. These sometimes splinter and may get lodged in the throat or may puncture the stomach or intestine.

PICA—Excessive Chewing and/or Eating of Undesirable Items

Dogs often chew on just about anything in sight, or have the bad habit of actually eating dirt, grass or even their own droppings. This problem is called coprophagy.

The problem of chewing is especially prevalent in young, teething puppies, and is usually outgrown by the time he reaches 8-10 months of age. Puppies will chew on wood, toys, articles of clothing, or anything else they can pick up or reach.

Several methods can be used to curb or prevent excessive chewing. If possible, items that the pups like to chew on should not be left in an area where they might be tempted. Discipline in the form of a swat with a rolled-up newspaper can also be used to put the point across in many instances. Since chewing is

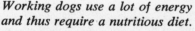

Working dogs use a lot of energy and thus require a nutritious diet.

a natural tendency of the pup, and most pups are quite active, it may be advisable to give him a plaything or something that he can chew on for his own. This can be a rawhide bone or a toy made especially for dogs. Bones can be used, although if they are, they should be the large round beef bones or the ox tails and not pork chop or chicken bones. Certain plastic toys are not suitable for puppies and can cause impactions if swallowed.

The problem of dogs eating dirt, wood, sand, and their own droppings, or other items, is believed to be caused by several factors including confinement and boredom. This problem is not unusual, especially in confined dogs, and not only will dogs chew on these items but may actually eat them. As mentioned, the main causes of dogs eating undesirable items seems to be confinement and boredom. This occurs at all ages and in any breed although it seems to be more prevalent in the working and hunting breeds.

Currently we do not know how to inhibit this habit nutritionally and have no evidence to indicate that it is related to diet. It can occur on any commercial dog food as well as on home-made rations.

Here again, providing something to play with or chew on, such as hardwood sticks or toys made for dogs, may be helpful. It may also be beneficial to give the dogs more exercise or a larger area in which to run. As the dog owner has probably noticed, when he is playing or exercising his dog, the problem of eating undesirable items does not occur.

Quite often this problem begins in winter when the droppings are frozen. Dogs that are on a limited feed intake or those not receiving enough food may develop this habit. Once a dog starts chewing on items, and especially their droppings, it seems to become a habit. One dog seeing another doing this often acquires the habit.

There is no specific remedy that can be used to prevent dogs from eating undesirable items. Disciplining the dog, removal of the various items from the area, if possible, or giving the dog more exercise or something to play with may be helpful. As far as stopping dogs from eating their droppings, we know of no specific remedy. Some people have used a veterinary product called Ectoral, which is given to the dog at a low level for a few days to impart a bad taste to the droppings. (Ectoral is also used to control external parasites in dogs.) Ectoral can be obtained through your veterinarian.

The dog should also be checked for parasites and any disease problem that might be present. Some people feel that these factors contribute to coprophagy.

If the dogs are looking for something to chew on or eat, keep dry dog food in a self-feeder or pan where they can reach it at all times. This provides them with something to do and keeps them occupied.

Something Snappy

To keep your dog out of waste baskets, garbage pails, and off chairs, set un-baited small mousetraps under paper in those locations. The snapping trap won't hurt a pup over Chihuahua size, but the noise will scare him.

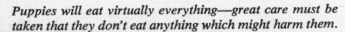

Puppies will eat virtually everything—great care must be taken that they don't eat anything which might harm them.

DIGESTIVE PROBLEMS*

IF your dog has regular or continuous problems, such as vomiting or diarrhea, unthriftiness or not holding his weight, seek the help of your veterinarian. Worms or infectious disease are sometimes responsible but your veterinarian is the best authority on the cause and what to do. You can do severe damage to your dog by experimenting on your own diagnosis and using do-it-yourself "cures." For example, there are many types of internal parasites and these must be controlled by more than one worming compound. Your veterinarian can make the diagnosis and prescribe the proper treatment.

VOMITING

The dog can vomit at will much easier than humans, to which anyone who has tried to give a dog a foul-tasting medicine can attest. Therefore, vomiting may merely show dislike. Grass, which dogs often like to eat, may cause the same thing.

A drastic change in diet may cause vomiting (or diarrhea). Whenever you anticipate a change, go slowly. Mix a small amount of the new food in with the former food. At each feeding, add a bit more of the new, decreasing the same amount of the old, until, within a couple of weeks, you have changed the diet gradually, and with no problems. Persistent vomiting, however, can be a symptom of some disorder. In that case, be sure to consult your veterinarian.

CONSTIPATION

An annoying and worrisome problem in dogs is constipation. This may be caused by an unbalanced diet, not enough water in the diet or by feeding too

*Feeding Research from the Purina Pet Center reprinted by permission.

Left—A drastic change in diet may cause vomiting or diarrhea. Dietary changes should be made gradually. Below—A German Shepherd puppy usually wants to know when chow time is coming. (Photo by Tom Morrissette.)

many bones, causing impaction. Older dogs commonly suffer from constipation, due to reduced activity and because their whole system is slowing down. Natural foods, such as liver, may be useful in relieving constipation or a dose of milk of magnesia will often be enough to take care of the problem. Here, again, if it continues, if the dog appears to be in pain or has other symptoms, he should be examined by your veterinarian. Don't experiment.

DIARRHEA

Although diarrhea is one of the symptoms of a number of disorders, it may be of temporary nature, and caused by improper feeding or diet. Many people neglect to follow feeding instructions on the labels of commercially produced foods and add excess milk, rich gravies or fats to the dog's food, causing diarrhea. Cow's milk, because of the lactose is not always easily digested by certain puppies and will cause diarrhea. The dry or evaporated milks, diluted with water, can usually be digested more easily. Raw eggs can also cause diarrhea.

If the diarrhea is only a slight occurrence, withhold food for awhile. It may be nothing more than an intestinal upset, caused by a change in diet, a change in drinking water (as when traveling), nervousness or fright. But if it continues, a dog soon becomes dehydrated. Any persistent case of diarrhea should be diagnosed by your veterinarian.

FLATULENCE

Indigestion is not always to blame when your dog passes foul-smelling gases. Usually the cause is feeding too much meat or too many eggs in the diet. Cut down on such foods and keep your dog on a complete diet. A charcoal tablet given every day or so may help until the condition clears up.

FEEDING FALLACIES

There are many "old-wives" tales about various foods being helpful or harmful. Here are just a few:

"Meat is dog's natural food."

False: In the wild state, the dog not only eats the flesh of the animal he kills for food but the mineral rich organs, and the grain and vegetable matter in the animal's digestive tract. He balances his own diet. In the home it is up to the owner to supply a balanced diet.

"Dogs need bones."

False: There is little in a bone that a dog's system needs, as long as he derives calcium from his regular food. While a puppy is teething (around 4 months of age) a large, tough bone with some meat on it is useful in getting rid of baby teeth. It relieves the puppy's urge to chew on everything in sight and keeps him pleasantly occupied. But, only large bones, such as beef knuckle or shank, should be given to dogs. The small, sharp bones of poultry or chops can splinter, damage the mouth and when swallowed may puncture the intestinal tract. An occasional bone of the right kind is all right and will help prevent tartar formation on the teeth but so will dry dog foods or biscuits. Too much bone chewing will wear the enamel off the teeth and too many hunks of bone in the digestive tract can cause constipation or serious impaction.

"Garlic will cure worms."

False: Generally the only effect garlic has on dogs is the same one it has on people. It practically insures privacy.

"Raw eggs will make the dog's coat shiny."

False: On the contrary, raw egg white interferes with the absorption of biotin, a vitamin needed for proper digestion. Eggs should be soft-boiled or otherwise cooked, if fed to dogs.

"A dog should chew his food."

False: "Wolfing" his food without chewing it is natural for the dog whose teeth are designed for tearing, not masticating, food. Almost all digestion takes place in the dog's stomach.

"Sugar causes worms."

False: Sugar or any other food does not "cause" worms. All digestible forms of carbohydrate are converted to simple sugars in the digestive tract. These are the dietary sugars that provide energy.

HEALTH

HEALTH GUIDE

A S WITH people, good health is a key factor to a happy life for dogs. It is quite a simple matter to spot a healthy dog—his coat shines, his eyes shine, he runs and plays, his nose is cold and wet and he is responsive and has a good appetite. But, does the opposite mean that the dog is sick? If he displays a few symptoms, does this mean that he is ill or that you should wait until all the symptoms appear before contacting the vet? Of course, these questions are asked slightly in jest. But, it is surprising how many dog owners are really quite unaware of their dog's state of health. Some owners fuss over every little itch, scratch, discharge, or growl while others are so insensitive that they fail to see problems until it is too late.

The purpose of this Health Guide section is to assist the typical dog owner in determining whether the dog's problem is out of the ordinary and demands the services of the vet, or if the situation can be handled calmly at home. It isn't necessary or wise to run to the vet with every slight problem, yet knowing where to draw the line is often difficult. That is where having some guide lines is helpful.

A dog will assume a typical and individual behavior pattern which is, after a short period of time, quite predictable. Dogs like to live by a regular routine and they will happily follow it daily. They like to eat and sleep according to this schedule. As a dog owner, you will soon become aware of your dog's habits and general normal behavior. It will, therefore, be quite obvious to you when there is a change in behavior.

Digestive Problems

Loss of Appetite

When food, which is usually gobbled down in one minute flat, is left untouched for hours, you know something is disturbing this usually ravenous canine. However, lack of appetite by itself is no cause for alarm. All dogs will at some time or other refuse to eat a meal or two. They should be allowed to do this without being pestered to eat or coaxed with tempting tidbits. The cause for this disinterest in food may be purely adjusting to overeating on previous days or to indigestion. Very often a dog will also eat grass, and then he will vomit. This is nature's way of curing an upset stomach. As mentioned previously, this is perfectly normal on occasion and should not be any reason for concern. However, should such poor eating habits or grass eating accompanied by vomiting occur more than once a week, then the dog's diet might be faulty and should be re-evaluated. If this persists after dietary changes, then an examination by the vet would be in order.

Vomiting

I. The habitual after meal vomiter

Some dogs who are healthy in every respect vomit quite regularly. This may be due to eating too rapidly and/or eating too much. These dogs will usually want to eat this regurgitated mass up again—there is nothing wrong with this, and they should be allowed to do so if they so desire. However, having such a mess regularly is not too pleasant especially when the dog lives in the house. It may be a relief to know that your dog isn't sick, but you will, in all probability, want to learn how to avoid this mess in the first place. Try these hints, and, if they don't help, consult your vet:

1—Let your dog rest about half an hour before feeding him.

2—Feed him in a quiet place away from the usual household commotion.

3—Feed him smaller portions—perhaps two small meals rather than one large one.

4—Let him rest after eating—avoid heavy exercise for at least half an hour.

II. Vomiting Yellow Stomach Juices.

Some dogs occasionally vomit stomach juices before their regular meal time. They will gag, ask to go out (if well trained) and then vomit a yellowy-foamy liquid. If this gets on carpeting, it makes quite a stain so wash it off immediately. As far as the dog is concerned, it is nothing to be overly concerned about. It's a build up of acid in the stomach when empty. This can sometimes be avoided by having a very regular meal time or by leaving a bowl with some dry kibble available at all times.

III. Continuous Vomiting.

An otherwise healthy appearing dog may start to vomit suddenly and continuously. If this vomiting continues and the dog can't keep anything down, then medical attention is required promptly. Excessive vomiting will cause dehydration, and, if this isn't treated, it can lead to death.

Puppies are particularly vulnerable to this type of situation. Like small children, they love to put things in their mouths and swallow them. Often, puppies will get something caught in their throat or lodged in their stomach, and this will cause the incessant vomiting. This misfortune can easily happen to a mature dog as well. That is why dog owners are cautioned not to give their dogs soft or small bones or rubber toys. These items, when chewed up, can create such a problem.

Constipation

This condition may be chronic or temporary. Insufficient exercise as well as the diet may be the cause. In chronic cases your vet may wish to examine the dog and prescribe a mode of treatment. When the problem is merely temporary, you might try giving your pet additional walks and exercise as well as some milk of magnesia or adding mineral oil to his food.

Diarrhea

Diarrhea is symptomatic of other problems. It may be caused by illness, intestinal parasites, or even emotional distress. The diarrhea can be treated, but the cause should be ascertained as well. Kaopectate can be administered. The quantity will depend on the size of the dog and the severity of the case. Check with your vet.

YOUR DOG'S COAT

Dogs of varying breeds possess a variety of coat types.

The long hairs of a dog's coat are cast regularly—twice during the year while the soft, multi-haired undercoat is cast a little at a time all the year round with a more pronounced moult in the spring. The main moult of long hair takes place in autumn. The incidence of coat casting is however open to a great many disturbing factors sometimes relating to general health or to hormone disturbances connected with whelping, oestrus and nutrition. Seasonal weather conditions also have an effect. Many smooth-coated white dogs, particularly Smooth Fox Terriers cast their long hairs throughout the year. With regular brushing this may not show a great deal on the body surface, while other breeds with longer hairs may be "out of coat" for a great portion of each year.

Some dogs have very "delicate" digestive systems and cannot tolerate rich food or certain types of table scraps. They must be maintained on specially prepared dog food in order to avoid any upset.

Nervous, high strung animals will react to an exciting or stressful situation by having diarrhea. This is particularly annoying to pet owners when it is uncontrollable and occurs in the house. Veterinarians often prescribe tranquilizers as well as special diets to calm these types. Puppies suffering from this nervous digestive disturbance are particularly difficult to housebreak. Tremendous patience is required to cope with this dilemma.

Skin Problems

Allergic

Allergic skin problems are sometimes called "Summer itch," eczema, or dermatitis. Dogs are prone to many allergic conditions with one of the more common manifestations of the allergy being via the skin. Many dogs suffer from itchy skin due to an allergy to grass, fungus found on grass, carpet, food, lawn food, weed killer, or even to laundry soap used on their bed or towel. With so many possibilities, it is virtually impossible to determine the exact cause of the dog's problem. These allergic skin attacks often occur only seasonally—the beginning of Spring, Summer, Winter, or Fall. They will return each year at roughly the same time. Once the vet has diagnosed the skin problem as having an allergic basis, treatment can be initiated; the successful treatment can be repeated on each occasion that the symptoms reappear.

Skin problems should be treated promptly, as delay means needless discomfort for the dog as well as damage to the dog's coat. Only very rarely will a skin condition improve without any treatment. It seems as though once an area has been sufficiently irritated, even if the original source of the irritation is removed, the dog will continue to scratch or bite that area. This is due to the fact that the original allergic skin lesion has now become infected as a result of the dog's scratching and biting. Therefore, clearing up both the allergy and the infection must be done in order to restore the dog to proper health. Some breeds are more susceptible to skin ailments than others.

Infections

Only your vet can determine if your dog's skin condition is allergic, infectious or whether it is caused by external parasites such as fleas, ticks, or mites. Often, he can find the cause of the problem only by a microscopic examination of skin scrapings from the affected area. Once he makes the diagnosis, he can prescribe the specific therapy needed. Antibiotics are often used to combat these skin infections.

Until proven otherwise, any skin disturbance can be contagious to other dogs and possibly to humans. It is wise to be cautious and to take special precautions. Keep the dog's bed clean, wash your hands carefully after touching the affected area, avoid contact with other dogs so as not to expose them, and then be sure to continue treatment until all traces of the problem are removed.

External Parasites

Frequently the dog's skin disturbance is caused by an external parasite.

I. Demodectic Mange (Red Mange)

This skin disturbance is caused by mites. Symptoms usually appear first around the eyes and mouth, and then they spread to other parts of the dog's body. Loss of hair occurs in patches. If left untreated, superinfections usually complicate the situation. Your vet will probably prescribe a skin cream or powder, oral medication, and possibly dips or baths. Young dogs and particularly those with short hair seem to be especially prone to this condition.

II. Sarcoptic Mange (Scabies)

This is another skin condition caused by mites which results in severe itching, hair loss, and crusty lesions. Treatment is very similar to that for Demodectic Mange. *This type of mange is contagious to people as well as other dogs.*

Ringworm

This is a highly communicable disease of the skin which can be transmitted from animal to man. Its appearance is that of a round sore with crusts or scabs, and it is caused by a fungus. The size and number of the sores increases as the disease progresses. In order to make an accurate diagnosis, it is necessary to have a microscopic examination.

Your veterinarian will undoubtedly prescribe the following treatment:
1—Clean infected spots—remove hair and crusts.
2—Apply a fungicide regularly until healing has occurred.
3—Keep lesions washed to avoid secondary infection.
4—Careful hygiene is essential to avoid spread.

Ear Mites

These mites confine themselves to the dog's outer ear. They are quite irritating, and, as a result, the dog will scratch his ears and shake his head. If not treated promptly, the dog can damage himself with his intense scratching. Your vet should be consulted in order to care for this delicate problem. Since this is quite contagious to other dogs, if you have more than one dog, you'll probably have more than one victim.

Fleas, Ticks, and Lice

Fleas are amazing pests and can move from host to host—going from dog to cat to man very easily. Frequent scratching, bald spots, and inflammation of the skin can signal an invasion of fleas. Visiting the vet for definite diagnosis and treatment is recommended. Powders, sprays, dips, specially treated collars, or even oral medication may be prescribed. At the same time, it is of utmost importance that the dog's living quarters be completely cleaned and sprayed. Frequent cleaning and vacuuming of the pet's area also helps to remove eggs, larvae, and pupae. Destroying the fleas not only relieves your animal's discomfort, it also reduces his likelihood of getting tapeworms, as their eggs are carried by fleas.

Ticks are picked up in the great outdoors from shrubbery and undergrowth. They are quite visible to the naked eye and should be watched for during grooming. Dipping your dog in a medicated solution is the usual method of treatment. Spraying and regular cleaning of the dog's sleeping quarters can aid in controlling this pest. Serious skin infections or paralysis can occur if ticks are not removed promptly. They are also carriers of other diseases (Rocky Mountain Spotted Fever is carried by several types of ticks)—another good reason to eliminate their presence.

Lice are not only aesthetically unpleasant, and therefore, not "nice," they can become a source of danger for your pet—especially if he happens to be a puppy. Often dogs with just a few lice are very "itchy," while those harboring thousands of lice may not scratch themselves at all. So small they escape notice, some lice penetrate the pet's skin and suck the blood. The females will lay eggs which in just three weeks will hatch and develop into adult lice. The constant blood-sucking, if extensive, can cause severe anemia in puppies and greatly weaken mature dogs, particularly females with nursing puppies. The pest

Flea Collars

Flea collars do a good job on fleas, but certain precautions need to be taken. After clipping or stripping, they may irritate the skin and should be removed for a few days. They have a bad effect in conjunction with anesthesia, so be certain to inform your veterinarian that your dog has been wearing one in case of surgery. Be certain never to use them in conjunction with any other insecticide or repellent.

can also be a source of irritation to cats and kittens. Your veterinarian is your best source of help.

Dandruff

Some dogs display a dry, scaly skin which may become a perfect site for a more malicious skin eruption. Opinion differs as to the cause for this dandruff. Neglect in terms of brushing, combing, and bathing

Dogs can suffer from eye problems if their long hair irritates their eyes.

has been suggested. More likely is excessive bathing with a drying type soap and/or living in an over-heated, overly-dry home. Additional brushing to stimulate the skin's natural oils is beneficial. Adding a special preparation to the diet and an oily dressing to the dog's coat can also be helpful.

Eye Problems

The eye is susceptible to a variety of problems. Foreign bodies can cause a slight irritation as well as serious damage. Symptoms of a problem in this area may be fluid running from the eye, as well as signs of distress, displayed by rubbing and pawing the irritated eye. Examine the eye and try to prevent the dog from doing additional injury to himself. Your vet can remove the foreign body and administer medication to combat infection. Any injury to the eye should be treated as rapidly as possible.

Infection

Symptoms of an eye infection are the same as those of a foreign body. Treatment usually involves administering an antibiotic eye ointment to the infected eye. Consult your vet.

Allergy

Allergic dogs usually have a variety of symptoms which may include not only the skin but also the eyes and nose. Itching, redness, discharge may all occur. Treatment with antihistamine (the same way doctors control hay fever) should help ease the animal's discomfort.

Cataracts and Blindness

Some breeds, because of excessive inbreeding, have developed a tendency to blindness and other visual problems. The best time to worry about this is *before* purchasing your puppy. Try to learn as much as possible about the breed which interests you, and if vision is a breed problem, try to be certain that there is no blindness in your pup's ancestors.

During old age, visual handicaps may develop in dogs of all breeds. Sometimes surgery can be of help. Usually blindness of old age comes on so gradually that the dog manages to compensate for his loss by using his other senses.

Blindness can be caused by specific illness, such as distemper, a serious eye infection, or an accident. Whether or not to destroy the dog with total blindness is a very personal decision.

Ear Problems

Infection

Symptoms of an ear infection may at first be rather generalized — little appetite, listlessness, whining.

When observed closely, they will give clues to their ear distress by rubbing the head on the ground and scratching and pawing at the throbbing ear as well as shaking the head. Your vet will be able to determine the necessary treatment.

Sometimes this condition is caused by a build up of natural wax plus grime. Ask your vet about cleaning your dog's ears. Some breeds require periodic ear cleaning.

Long-eared dogs seem to be particularly susceptible to ear infections because moisture doesn't have a good opportunity to dry, making it a fine spot for germs to proliferate. This is why extreme care should be taken when bathing a long-eared dog. Cotton should be inserted before the bath and the ears should be thoroughly dried after the bath. Another difficulty experienced by long-eared breeds is that the ears get soiled and become a fine culture media. Checking the ears frequently and keeping them clean is good hygiene.

Deafness

A small percentage of dogs are deaf from birth on. This is the reason for checking the hearing prior to purchase. Deafness in a puppy is probably a birth defect. Certain breeds have a predisposition toward deafness, thus, careful breeding practices should be followed. Deafness can also be caused by illness and by accidents. Prompt health care can prevent unnecessary difficulties.

Old age—the villain—may also cause deafness. But, if watched carefully and directed by hand signals rather than voice signals, the older dog with a hearing loss can still continue to function.

Tumors

Tumors, both malignant and benign, are to be found in dogs. If you become aware of any lumps or swellings consult the vet promptly. Early detection and modern surgery have made tumors less dreaded. Unspayed females are most vulnerable to tumors. A wise idea is to have your veterinarian give your pet a yearly complete check-up after the age of five.

Fits

Fits are muscular tremors which appear suddenly. They may be caused by illness, poisoning, or by emotional upset. It is best to allow the dog to calm down and to consult the vet.

Dog Psychiatry

Psychiatrists and psychologists are accepted in the area of human mental health care. Presently this is not the case in the dog world. Although there is an increased awareness of a "need" in this area there are still very few trained people to help the emotionally disturbed dog.

The study of doggy emotions is not new. Just as other animals, such as mice and rats, have been used in the psychology lab so the dog has also been studied. (Remember Pavlov's dog?) It has been found that dogs are prone to many of the disturbances seen in humans, such as neurosis, psychosis, and hysteria. Emotional problems may be exhibited by:

(1) **Severe nervousness**—a dog that is tense, anxious, can't relax, barks excessively, is always watching or prowling, won't allow himself to be touched or to play and relax is definitely abnormal. A pet displaying such a mode of behavior is difficult to live with and gives his owners little enjoyment.

(2) **The compulsive barker**—this dog barks continuously or frequently for no obvious reason. This is most annoying and disturbing to all those around him.

(3) **The fear-biter**—a most dangerous dog to keep because of the distinct possibility that he will injure someone. Dogs that have suffered some traumatic experience may respond to any fearful situation by attacking and biting.

(4) **Shyness and withdrawal**—this problem can be readily identified, a dog that hangs back or hides when greeted, or approaches people with his tail tucked between his legs and his head down is definitely suffering from this disturbance.

(5) **The sexual offender**—a male dog who masturbates excessively and who disturbs children and visitors with his behavior presents a definite problem.

(6) **The aggressive and hostile dog**—this type of animal is usually impossible to maintain in a regular home setting unless helped. A dog that attacks others or severely frightens them is not only suffering from a problem but is most certainly creating one for his owner.

These are a few examples of disturbed dogs that would need psychiatric help. Presently there are very few veterinarians available who can "treat" these problems. We know of a clinic in California that treats the disturbed dogs belonging to movie stars. However, there are more dogs with "problems" than there are professionals to treat them. The solution at the present time would seem to be to follow many of the suggestions for good mental health recommended for our own human population:

(1) Provide a happy, loving home.
(2) Keep stress and tension at a minimum.
(3) Prevent bad habits from forming—firmness not permissiveness.
(4) Have clear, well defined rules and limits and be consistent.
(5) Never allow cruelty to be inflicted.
(6) Don't breed a dog that shows personality deviations. (Unfortunately humans have not yet

attained this level of wisdom).

(7) Seek professional help when necessary.

Infectious Diseases

Canine Distemper

This is probably the most dreaded disease in the dog world. Statistics show that half of the dogs which contract distemper will die; the death rate among puppies sometimes reaches 80 per cent. Survivors of distemper are often left with damage to their nervous system or to their sense of smell, sight, or hearing. Partial or total paralysis is not unusual.

Canine distemper is an infectious disease. It is not necessary that a healthy dog come in contact with a diseased dog to become infected. The virus may be borne by air currents and inanimate objects. This, of course, increases the dangers of the disease since it virtually makes all susceptible dogs vulnerable to an attack. Canine distemper is found also in foxes, wolves and mink but not in cats. Canine hepatitis, another serious illness of dogs, often occurs simultaneously with canine distemper. Neither distemper nor canine hepatitis is transmissible to man.

The many signs of distemper are not always typical and for this reason treatment may be delayed or neglected. Usually the animal is listless and has a poor appetite. Congestion of the eyes may cause squinting or discharge. Cough, nasal discharge and diarrhea are

Sadness is a sick dog. (Photo by Maia Coven.)

CANINE DISTEMPER

Canine distemper is the greatest single disease threat to the canine population. At least half of the dogs contracting distemper will die; the death rate sometimes reaches 80 percent among pups.

---

common. The virus may attack the nervous system, causing partial or complete paralysis, "fits," or a twitching in groups of muscles. Distemper is so prevalent and the symptoms so varied that any sick young dog should be taken immediately to your veterinarian for a definite diagnosis.

Practically speaking, it is nearly impossible to prevent exposure to canine distemper virus. Young dogs are more susceptible to the disease than older ones. However, some mature dogs leading comparatively isolated lives are very susceptible to the disease because they have not been recently exposed to the virus. This susceptibility may exist even though they were vaccinated when very young. No dog should be admitted into an area of possible exposure to distemper without immediate vaccination, unless it has been vaccinated within the last 12 months.

It is clear, therefore, that vaccination of your pet against canine distemper is not only highly recommended, but imperative.

Immunization against canine distemper provides the only effective means of control of the disease in the dog population. Since lasting protection, unfortunately, cannot be guaranteed as the result of a single series of inoculations, annual re-vaccination is strongly recommended.

Pups older than three to four months that have an unknown immune status should receive at least one dose of modified live virus vaccine. Younger pups should get at least two doses, the first one after weaning and the last at 12 to 16 weeks of age. Some authorities hold that vaccination should be commenced at six to eight weeks of age and then repeated every two weeks until the pup is three or four months of age. These regional variations in vaccination procedure are dictated by the infectivity of the distemper virus in a given area.

It is impossible for the average pet owner to determine the correct time for vaccination. This is a matter which requires the good professional judgment of your veterinarian, based on his experience and the general health of the dog.

The important thing to remember is that veterinarians are now able to provide most dogs with complete protection against canine distemper.

Rabies

Rabies remains a public health problem even though there have been few human fatalities recently. All warm-blooded animals can spread rabies—the majority of the animal rabies cases in the United States are found in wildlife such as skunk, foxes, and bats. Dogs and cats are the most commonly infected domestic pets. Thus, every pet owner has the responsibility of inoculating his animal in order to prevent rabies outbreaks.

Rabies is transmitted from animals to man by a bite from the infected animal. Everyone bitten by a domestic or wild animal need not undergo antirabies vaccinations. Following a bite, however, a physician should be consulted immediately. The animal should be confined by a veterinarian and observed for 14 days. If the animal remains well at the end of this period, then the rabies virus is not present. Confinement is necessary even for vaccinated dogs because the vaccine is only about 80 per cent effective. However, if rabies symptoms appear, then the administration of antirabies vaccine becomes necessary. The American Veterinary Medical Association makes the following suggestions to prevent rabies:

First of all, have your pet vaccinated if you haven't already done so. Veterinary medical scientists have developed safe and effective vaccines which give your pet maximum protection against rabies. To insure continued maximum protection, follow your veterinarian's advice and observe your local rabies control regulations.

Second, if bitten by an animal, thoroughly cleanse the wound with soap and irrigate with profuse quantities of running warm water. Contact your physician, Board of Health, or police department immediately. *Confine, do not kill the animal.*

Third, obey leash and licensing laws in your community.

Fourth, make sure your pet is identified by a license tag and a rabies inoculation tag.

Fifth, report stray dogs to the police or local pound department.

Finally, teach children not to play with strange pets and to avoid handling any wild animal, particularly when it appears to be tame. This is especially important when you are camping.

Leptospirosis

The organisms responsbile for leptospirosis are transmitted by the feces or urine of infected rats. In areas where rats are present, it is imperative that the dog's food be kept well-sealed so that it cannot be contaminated.

Symptoms of the disease are: vomiting, fever, diarrhea, jaundice, loss of appetite, and depression. Prompt veterinary attention is mandatory.

Prevention of the disease is now possible by vaccination. A yearly booster is recommended to maintain a good level of immunity.

Infectious Hepatitis

Infectious hepatitis is a viral disease which attacks the liver. Transmission is via the urine of infected dogs or viral carriers.

Symptoms are quite similar to distemper—fever, vomiting, diarrhea, pain, and anemia. This disease is often fatal.

A preventative vaccine is now available; and, there is a triple booster for distemper, hepatitis, and leptospirosis.

Coughs, Colds, Tonsillitis, Bronchospasms

Dogs kept in kennels are prone to a condition known as "kennel cough" which is a dry, gagging cough caused by an infection. Except for the cough, there usually aren't any other symptoms. Dog cough syrup may be used to relieve the soreness of the throat.

Coughing can also be caused by something caught in the throat. If you suspect this possibility, an X-ray may be necessary.

Many other conditions are characterized by coughs such as upper respiratory infections, distemper, sore throat, tonsillitis, pneumonia, heartworm, and asthma. Only your veterinarian can make a definitive diagnosis.

Manifestations of a cold may occur at any time. Symptoms are a watery discharge from the nose, possibly also from the eyes, listlessness and loss of appetite. Aspirin can help to reduce the discomfort.

Excessive licking of the lips is the most common sign of a sore throat and possible tonsillitis. Your vet can prescribe medication for this condition.

Bronchospasms may be allergic—consult your vet.

Stolen Dogs

Police departments and humane societies estimate that nearly 1 million dogs are stolen every year in the U.S. Many of these are stolen from autos that are left unlocked, or with the windows open, at shopping centers, restaurants, sports stadiums, recreation parks, fishing docks, etc.

Two mature Shetland Sheepdogs—the dog on the right had rickets, caused by a dietary deficiency, as a puppy.

Dietary Deficiencies

Rickets

Rickets is a disease affecting the bones and teeth of puppies caused by a deficiency of vitamin D, calcium, and phosphorus. Proper diet, adequate sunshine, and vitamins can reverse this disease if treated in time. Symptoms of the disease are bowed legs, weak muscles, deformed joints, lack of vigor, arched neck, and a poor stance.

It is of utmost importance that bitches in pregnancy and lactation have sufficiently high amounts of vitamin D, calcium, and phosphorus. This is important both for maintaining their own health and for the proper formation of their puppies.

Black Tongue

Black tongue is a vitamin B complex deficiency disease which will not occur in dogs maintained on a good diet. It is not infectious or contagious. Treatment is only effective if the diet is corrected and nutritious foods high in the B vitamins are added, such as meat, milk, eggs, and liver.

Internal Parasites

Worming of Dogs

Dogs can be infested with different species of worms, including roundworms, hookworms, heartworms, tapeworms, and whipworms. Just as in poultry and livestock operations, worms can cause many dollars worth of damage in a kennel or breeding operation. Pups are most severely affected, with symptoms appearing as poor growth, rough hair coat, diarrhea, listlessness, and if the infection is severe death may occur.

In addition, roundworms and hookworms present a public health problem since the larvae from these species can infect humans.

All dogs should routinely have their droppings checked for the presence of worms by a veterinarian. Brood females should be wormed or checked prior to or within three weeks after breeding. Hookworm and roundworm larvae can pass from the dam via the bloodstream through the placenta to developing pups As a result, if the dam is infected, pups can be heavily infested with these species at birth.

Pups in good health can be wormed at four to five weeks of age if necessary. If dogs are heavily infested, worming should be repeated in three to four weeks. This is necessary since the life cycle of most worms is such that part of their life is spent in parts of the body other than the intestines. Even though worms are removed from he intestine the individual worms in the rest of the body soon mature and migrate to the intestines. This can be controlled by worming dogs periodically. Normally no problems occur if a reputable product is used and directions for treatment are followed. Never worm sick or weak dogs recently exposed to disease unless under veterinary supervision.

Hookworm eggs can be destroyed in dog runs by sprinkling a saturated salt solution over the area at a rate of one gallon per 100 square feet or sprinkling three pounds of dry sodium borate per gallon of water over the same amount of area. Both salt and borate destroy the eggs by dessication, or drawing the moisture out of the cell. Remember, salt is harmful to vegetation and care should be taken in its application. This treatment is effective against hookworm eggs only.

Roundworms

One of the most important parasites in dogs is the large intestinal roundworm (*Ascarids*). These white or yellowish colored worms, when mature, will measure two to eight inches in length.

The presence of roundworms in the intestines of a young dog is characterized by marked enlargement of the abdomen, unthriftiness, listlessness, and may be accompanied by digestive disturbances. If the infection is heavy or severe, worms may even be passed in the dog's droppings or in the vomit the dog produces when he coughs. The coughing is most prevalent when the larvae are passing through the lungs. When large numbers of larvae are present in the lungs, pneumonia may develop.

Many times it appears that adult dogs may develop an immunity against roundworms; therefore, it is a less serious problem in mature dogs than it is in young pups. However, roundworms can still be present in adult dogs and unless they are treated, the adult dogs will spread the worms to other dogs.

Just as the hookworm larva, the roundworm larva

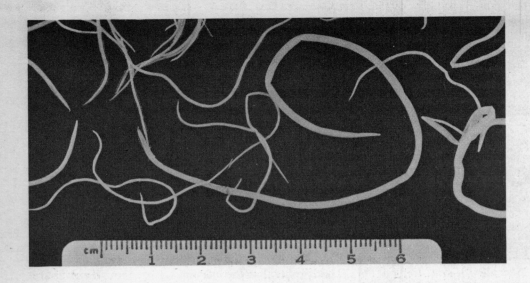

ROUNDWORMS — the larvae of this parasite can present a public health problem since it can invade the human body.

can migrate through the blood system of the pregnant mother to her developing pups, and consequently, the pups may be heavily infected with worms at birth. This emphasizes the importance of worming the pregnant female early (at least the first three weeks) in her gestation period or even prior to breeding.

The larvae of the roundworm present a public health problem, since the Ascarid larvae can invade the body of humans and cause a condition known as visceral larva migrans. Generally, this disease develops in children less than three years of age, due to their habits of putting their fingers in their mouth, or eating dirt which may be contaminated.

There are many good roundworm treatments available, some of which contain piperazine. If this compound is used, the dog does not have to be fasted since the medication can be given right in his food.

Hookworm

The most injurious internal parasites in puppies are hookworms. These worms are common and can be found in dogs in most sections of the country. They are grayish-white in color, ½- to ¾-inch in length and as thick as a straight pin. These worms attach themselves with teeth or cutting blades to the lining of the mucosa of the dog's small intestine.

There are three kinds of hookworms; all have similar life cycles. The adult female worms attached to the small intestine deposit a large number of eggs which pass in the dog's droppings. If there is ample moisture available and a temperature of 72-86 deg. F, these eggs hatch in 12-24 hours. Extreme dryness as well as freezing temperatures kill the freshly hatched larvae. For this reason, the incidence and severity of hookworm infection is lowest during mid-Winter and highest in the Summer.

The larvae develop to a third or infective stage in a week, at which time they are picked up directly by the dog in contaminated feed, water, or when the dog licks any portions of his body that may have worm eggs clinging to it. The larvae go directly to the small intestine where they mature to adults. The infective

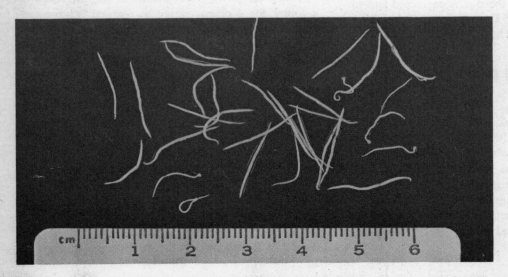

HOOKWORMS—the most injurious parasite in puppies. Heavy infestation can cause anemia or even death in young dogs.

larvae can also penetrate the dog's skin, going first into the blood stream and then into the lungs. In the lungs they are coughed up, swallowed and go to the small intestine.

Prenatal infection can occur in females during the gestation period. The migrating larvae go from the female via the blood stream to the placenta and pass into the developing young. Consequently, pups are sometimes heavily infected at birth. The main effects of hookworm on dogs, and the condition which makes them so serious, is the heavy blood loss they can cause. An infected dog may have continuous bloody diarrhea from persistent hemorrhaging caused by the hookworms in the intestine. In young dogs this can cause anemia or may even result in death. Many times young puppies that are heavily infected and treated properly may even be given a blood transfusion to help overcome the anemia. Failure to treat heavy hookworm infection will usually result in death of the pup. To illustrate the high blood loss, if there are 100 adult worms in the small intestine, it is estimated that these worms will take up as much as .25-.4 oz. of blood every 24 hours. It is easy to imagine what can happen if there would be several hundred worms present.

Symptoms of hookworm infection are poor stamina and general poor growth of the dog, along with the presence of blood in the droppings. If worms are present, the eggs or even some of the worms may be found in the droppings. The presence of hookworms can be determined by having your veterinarian check a droppings sample.

Diagnosis and treatment for hookworm should be done by your veterinarian. There are many wormers available which can be used in the treatment of hookworms, including pills or capsules and a wormer which is injected into the dog's subcutaneous tissue.

Tapeworms

There are at least 14 different species of tapeworms that can infect dogs in this country. Some of these species are limited to certain areas, but all depend upon suitable insects or other intermediate hosts to complete their life cycle.

Tapeworms vary in size from a fraction of an inch up to 30 feet depending upon the species and age of the worm. Intermediate hosts such as fleas, lice, rodents (rats, rabbits, mice), fish, and snakes are necessary in order for each specie of worm to complete its life cycle. Infection of the dog with a particular specie of tapeworm depends on the one present in the area and the intermediate host that the dog swallows or eats. If the intermediate host happens to be a flea or biting louse which the dog swallows, then he will pick up the larval stage of the particular species of the parasite this host is carrying. Other species can be picked up by the dog eating the intestines of rabbits, or the livers of rats or mice in which the immature stages of the worm are found.

Symptoms of tapeworm infestation in dogs are: digestive disturbances, abdominal pain, nervousness, and unthriftiness. Animals with mild cases probably suffer only abdominal discomfort and the inexperienced dog owner may not notice this. Heavy tapeworm infection may show up as persistent or alternating diarrhea and/or constipation. An important factor regarding tapeworms in dogs is that they may pass in the droppings and can, through the intermediate host, infest other livestock and man. The tapeworm segments passing in the droppings of infected dogs can contaminate furniture, dog bedding, and may even soil these items. The segments have a pinkish tinge when fresh, but are brown when dry and look like grains of rice.

TAPEWORM—transmitted through an intermediate host, the tapeworm can vary in size from a fraction of an inch to 30 feet depending on species and age.

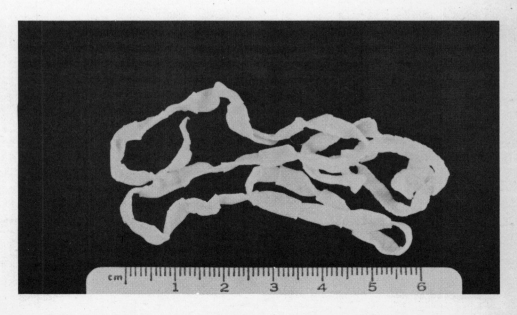

A dog infected with tapeworms may occasionally be seen sitting down and dragging his hind quarters over the floor or ground. This is partly attributable to the irritation that the segments cause when they pass through the intestines. The tapeworm can be detected by observing their segments in the dog's droppings. Also, if the veterinarian is given a sample of the dog's droppings, he can detect worm segments under a microscope, if they are present.

Treatment for tapeworm is by giving the dog a wormer designed for use against this parasite. Your veterinarian can give you information as to the most effective wormer for the particular species of worm which your dog may have.

Try to prevent your dog from coming in contact with the worm or intermediate host of a particular species of tapeworm. This can be done by controlling the rodent population around your area, and keeping your dog free of external parasites. As with most health problems, good management and prompt treatment upon diagnosis are necessary to help eliminate tapeworms in your dog.

Heartworm

One of the most difficult internal parasites to treat in dogs is the heartworm. This worm is most prevalent along the coastal areas of the United States although it is also found in the central and northern regions. The adult worm is slender, measuring ten to 12 inches in length with the female worm usually longer than the male. The adult worms most frequently live in the right ventricle of the heart.

The adult heartworm releases embryos or young worms, known as microfilariae, into the blood stream. These microfilariae circulate in the blood and do not develop further until they are ingested by a suitable intermediate host. This host is usually the mosquito although it has been found that fleas may also spread them. This is one reason for the high incidence of heartworms around the sea coast. When the mosquito takes in a small amount of blood containing the microfilariae the organism develops further in the insect's body. Complete embryonzation takes ten to 14 days at which time the microfilariae emerge as larvae. When the mosquito again feeds on another dog, this larvae can be transferred to the animal being fed upon. From this point there is little known about the remainder of the life cycle. It is thought that the larva migrates to certain connective tissue in the body and with the completion of the intermediate development, proceeds to the right ventricle by way of the veins. This completion of the life cycle may take three to four months from the time the young worm first enters the dog's body.

Signs of heartworm infection include a chronic cough and lack of stamina, especially after exercise. The presence of a large number of heartworms in the right ventricle can cause heart enlargement and subsequent heart damage. Continued infection can produce a strain on the heart which may eventually result in death of the dog.

Diagnosis of the presence or absence of microfilariae is made by observing a blood sample under the microscope. If microfilariae are present this indicates there are adult worms in the heart.

To date no single medication does a completely satisfactory job of treating both the larva and the adult heartworm. Surgery has been used to remove adult worms. Many of the wormers now available contain arsenicals which are effective in heartworm treatment. Treatment is difficult, not because the worms are hard to kill but from possible after effects. If all of the worms are killed at once there is a possibility that a clump of them may lodge in a major

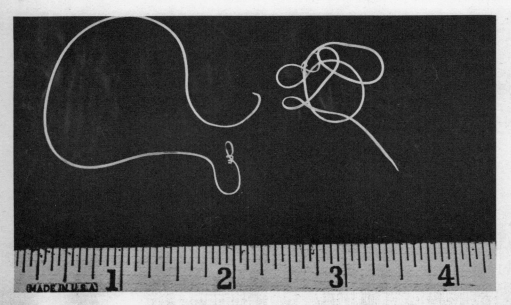

HEARTWORMS — one of the most difficult internal parasites in dogs to treat, the adult heartworm usually lives in the right ventricle of the host dog's heart.

blood vessel and cause death. Therefore, the worms should be killed a few at a time to prevent an accumulation. If an accumulation of dead worms occurs in the blood vessels of the lungs, pneumonia may result. Diagnosis for heartworms, and treatment if any are found, should be done by a veterinarian. The treatment period will usually be long and during this time the dog should have ample rest.

The best method for preventing recurrence of heartworms is to keep down the number of mosquitos in your area and prompt treatment of any infected dog. If heartworms prevail in your area, keep your home or kennel area screened so that the dog has minimum exposure to mosquitos. Drain all marsh lands and still water areas which are not in use as an aid in preventing mosquitos from hatching. Another manner for the prevention of infestation necessitates giving medicine daily during the mosquito season and for two months after a killing frost. The medicine is given only to dogs that have a negative blood test. This medicine destroys the microfilaria that may be introduced by mosquitos. Semi-annual blood tests for all dogs, preferably in March and November, are recommended.

Whipworms

Whipworms that are found in dogs have a white or gray colored whip-like body and are two to three inches long at maturity. They are usually found in the cecum (a blind pouch located between the large and small intestines) of the dog. The dog is infected by swallowing embryonated eggs picked up in contaminated water, feed, or by licking off eggs that may be clinging to his hair coat. The swallowed embryonated eggs hatch in the small intestine and in two to three months the young worms travel to the cecum.

Little is known about the damage whipworms cause to dogs. Symptoms of severe infection are chronic diarrhea, abdominal pain, prolonged nervousness, unthriftiness, and frequent periods of constipation and diarrhea. If diarrhea persists, blood may show up in the droppings. Animals affected with severe cases of whipworm may die if left untreated.

Identification of the worm can be made by a veterinarian upon microscopic examination of the droppings for whipworm eggs. Treatment is by a wormer designed for whipworm control. This wormer can be obtained from your veterinarian.

Routine checking of dropping samples for whipworms, prompt treatment if any are found, and good sanitation of the area in which the dog lives do much to prevent further spread and also aids in the elimination of these internal parasites.

Worming Precautions

The following precautions should be followed when worming your dog. Always follow the worming directions specifically. Dogs which are sick, weak or exposed to a disease, such as distemper, should not be wormed except under specific supervision of the veterinarian. Cleanliness of the dog and his kennel is a must for good worm control.

WHIPWORMS—little is known about the damage these parasites cause, however, symptoms of infection include diarrhea, abdominal pain, and nervousness.

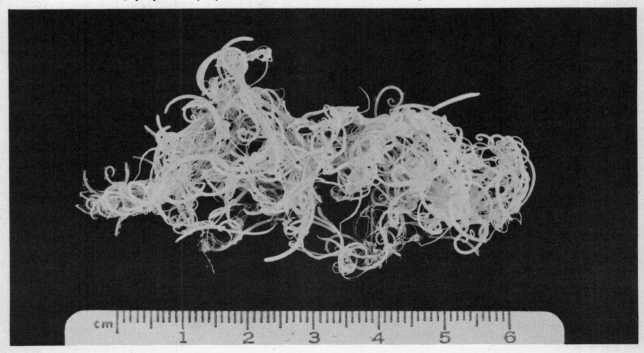

SOME ORTHOPEDIC PROBLEMS

Osteochondritis Dissecans
As A Cause of Shoulder Lameness in the Big Dog

Sudden forelimb lameness in the juvenile dog of the larger breeds may be a manifestation of osteochondritis dissecans, an increasingly diagnosed condition of the shoulder joint.

The disease has been reported as occurring most frequently in large and giant breeds between the ages of 5 and 12 months, a time at which the skeletal system is most susceptible to injury. A typical history of lameness after strenuous exercise of sudden stops in front of fences, and in connection with training or jumping is common.

The symptoms of lameness, refusal to use the affected limb, painful resistance to full extension of the forelimb and atrophy of the shoulder muscles are common findings. These symptoms are the result of an injury to the subchondral bone and cartilage of the shoulder joint. Pathologically, these lesions are seen as a bone necrosis of the central portion of the humeral articular surface with discoid plaques of cartilage at the site of injury.

A diagnosis of osteochondritis dissecans is most often made by the clinical symptoms of shoulder lameness after strenuous exercise. Radiographic diagnosis is helpful in severe or long standing cases, but in the acute stage lesions may not be apparent radiographically.

Fortunately, most dogs afflicted will make a functional recovery with rest and restricted exercise. Some veterinarians have used intra-articular injections of steriods to shorten the recovery period. More persistent cases of the disease may require surgical intervention to remove the bony lesion or pieces of detached cartilage within the joint capsule.

Although osteochondritis dissecans is more prevalent in some breeds and in some lines than others, breeders, trainers and large dog fanciers can help prevent this condition by exercising judgment in the amount of exercise a juvenile is allowed during this critical period of his development.

Canine Elbow Dysplasia

Elbow dysplasia is a descriptive term applied to a developmental abnormality of the elbow joint that is manifested by bony changes and foreleg lameness. Elbow dysplasia has been described in the German Shepherd Dog, St. Bernards, Irish Wolfhounds, Basset Hounds, Newfoundlands, Bloodhounds, Labrador Retrievers and Great Danes. This disease has been diagnosed in dogs ranging in age from three and a half months to three years, with six months the most frequently reported age of diagnosis. Elbow dysplasia has not been reported in the small breeds of dogs.

Clinical signs of the disease vary from slight lameness to refusal to bear weight on the affected limb. The lameness generally is gradual in appearance, inter-

---

CANINE PANOSTEITIS

Panosteitis is a disease of unknown origin which causes pain and lameness primarily in young growing dogs of the larger breeds. The disease has also been termed enostosis and eosinophilic panosteitis. Panosteitis has been reported in several breeds of dogs including the German Shepherd Dog, St. Bernard, Basset Hound, Great Dane, Doberman Pinscher, German Shorthaired Pointer, Irish Setter, Airedale Terrier, Samoyed and Miniature Schnauzer. Male dogs are more often affected and the condition is most frequently diagnosed between five and 13 months of age. Typical signs of the disease are a lameness which may affect one or more legs and shift from limb to limb intermittently over a period of several weeks. This lameness is usually not associated with injury. Diminished appetite and activity are common findings. Localized pain in the long bones of the legs can usually be demonstrated by firm pressure over the affected area. In the middle phase of the disease, diagnosis of panosteitis can be made radiographically. Characteristic radio-dense, patchy areas appear in the medullary canal of the long bones such as the humerus, femur, tibia, radius and ulna. Radiography is the most reliable means of differentiating lameness caused by panosteitis from other juvenile lameness such as hip dysplasia, elbow dysplasia or osteochondritis dissecans. The lameness caused by panosteitis is self-limiting and symptoms usually abate with time. Treatment with aspirin, corticosteroids have been helpful in the relief of pain associated with this condition.

mittent in nature and may become more pronounced after exercise. A frequent complaint is lack of drive in gaiting and loss of stamina. One leg or both forelegs may be affected. Severely affected dogs stand with bowed elbows and have swollen joints with increased joint fluid. These dogs resent forced movement of the elbow joint.

The diagnosis of elbow dysplasia is based on radiographic findings of an ununited anconeal process (which is a loose fragment of bone in the posterior portion of the elbow joint) and/or early osteoarthritis of the elbow with the arm flexed is a diagnostic clue for the observation of the anconeal process. Care must be taken in viewing radiographs of large dogs under 140 days of age since normal bony union is not complete until after this time.

Treatment of this condition is aimed at relief of pain by surgically removing the loose bone fragment within the elbow joint before osteoarthritic changes become aggravated. Experimental trial breeding of dogs with elbow dysplasia indicate the condition to be an inherited trait with a strong familial tendency. The mode of inheritance is thought to be that of three dominant genes controlling the appearance of the disease.

Since elbow dysplasia is an inherited abnormality, affected dogs should not be considered for breeding. Dogs with elbow dysplasia should be removed from breeding programs and preferably neutered for use as pet animals. Surgical removal of the ununited anconeal process has been useful in the relief of pain and lameness associated with the disease.

OTHER HEALTH HINTS

Taking a Dog's Temperature

There will be times when you may believe your dog is sick and has a fever. Possible clues that can signal the existence of a temperature are: (1) Heavy panting, (2) a hot, dry nose. The only way to know for certain whether the dog is sick is to take his temperature. The procedure is actually quite simple, but it must be done carefully to avoid accidentally injuring the dog:

• Use a rectal thermometer.
• Shake down the mercury.
• Apply some vaseline or other lubricant to the tip.
• Hold the dog in a standing position.
  Speak reassuringly to the dog while holding him.
• Insert thermometer gently and slowly into the rectum.
• Wait about three minutes and then remove gently.
• Normal temperature of dogs is 101 deg. to 101.5 deg. F.
• Any significant rise in temperature above this is a sign of illness. Consult your vet.

When to See the Vet

The American Veterinary Medical Association suggests you consult your veterinarian if your pet shows any of the following symptoms:

1—Abnormal behavior, sudden viciousness or lethargy.
2—Abnormal discharges from the nose, eyes, or other body openings.
3—Abnormal lumps, limping, or difficulty getting up or lying down.
4—Loss of appetite, marked weight losses or gains, or excessive water consumption. Difficult, abnormal, or uncontrolled waste elimination.
5—Excessive head shaking, scratching, and licking or biting any part of the body.
6—Dandruff, loss of hair, open sores, and a ragged or dull coat. Foul breath or excessive tartar deposits on teeth.

Choosing Your Veterinarian

If you are fortunate enough to live in an area served by more than one veterinarian, you will have the choice of selecting one. For many ardent pet owners this choice ranks in importance with the choice of the family doctor. Certainly you must consider proximity and availability as well as finding someone in whom you can have complete trust and confidence. Veterinarians are highly trained professional people who have devoted years of study in preparing for this field. All veterinarians are required to have a minimum of two years of pre-veterinary college study prior to four years of professional study in a college of veterinary medicine. Subsequent passing of a state board examination is required to be licensed to practice in any state or province. Thus, your pet should be in good hands and should receive the finest care available today.

Administering Medication

At some time or other your dog will have to take medicine. The easiest way is the best way! Attitude is most important, and your dog can sense it if you feel that you are going to do something unpleasant. Pretending that you have a great surprise will enlist his interest.

I. Giving Capsules and Pills

There are two ways to go about this—the professional way and the fun way.

The professional way involves holding the dog's upper jaw with one hand and pressing his cheeks inward to cover the teeth and pushing the capsule far back in the throat with the other hand. Then, closing his mouth with both hands and stroking his throat gently to make him swallow.

The fun and easy way is to wrap the pill or capsule in a small amount of liver sausage and watch the whole thing disappear in one bite. It's a pleasure to see the grateful look and to have him come running the next time it's pill time.

II. Giving Liquid Medicine

With a stubborn dog this is no easy trick. Most sources simply say to pull out the dog's lower lip to form a pocket and then to pour the liquid into this pocket with a spoon or dropper. Perhaps after doing this hundreds of times one becomes proficient. The typical pet owner, however, may find that giving liquid medicine is quite difficult. A quick shake of the dog's head and you are left standing there covered with medicine. We have found it necessary to be well covered before attempting this stunt. Our greatest success has come by mixing the liquid medicine into a taste tempting meal, i.e. liver and broth or chicken giblets au jus.

Care of the Recuperating Dog

When your pet is ill, he needs your love, care, and attention more than ever. That is why most animal authorities recommend nursing your dog back to health at home rather than in the animal hospital. By all means visit the veterinarian, have the dog examined and medication and treatment prescribed, but then take him home and let him recuperate in his own familiar surroundings with his own "family." You will have more patience in coaxing his reluctant appetite and more ability in cheering him up. That personal, warm touch will mean a faster and happier recovery.

Just remember to follow the veterinarian's directions and to give all the medication and treatment as prescribed. Call the vet if there are any changes in the dog's symptoms. If these steps are followed, the recovery should be rapid.

Heavy panting and a hot, dry nose are clues to the existence of a fever in a dog. The only way to be certain, however, is to take the dog's temperature.

KNOWING WHAT'S NORMAL IS VITAL

Determining the state of your dog's health can be difficult unless you know whether or not his outward signs are normal. But to know what is *abnormal* you must first know what is *normal*.

Temperature: a quiet, calm dog's temperature ranges from 100.5 to 101.5 degrees Fahrenheit. A normal rise of two degrees may be caused by excitement, activity, a hot room, or the sun. A bitch's temperature will drop two or three degrees from 12 to 24 hours before whelping.

Respiration: The normal rate of respiration is between 18 to 28 per minute. Rapid breathing when the dog has been quiet may very well indicate trouble, as may mouth-breathing at rest.

Heart: At rest the normal heart beat ranges from 90 to 100 beats per minute (faster in puppies and older dogs). Also a resting dog's heart normally has an irregular beat (it beats faster on inspiration and slower on expiration). A regular beat in a quiet dog may indicate heart trouble. The heartbeat can be felt rather easily through the chest wall just behind the front legs; also by feeling the inner side of the hind leg. When it is difficult to locate, press your ear to the dog's chest. Puppies born with a very slow heart-rate seldom survive.

Eyes: The white on the top half of the eye should be bright and clear, with a few small vessels. Excitement and activity will cause more vessels to be noticeable. But if the upper half is too white the dog may be anemic. The lower half of the eyeball should be a bright, healthy pink. The cornea (the clear part) should be bright, glistening and perfectly clear.

Ears: The inside of the ear should be smooth and pink under the hair, with the canal perfectly clean (without attention from you), very smooth, and a pale pink. Dust and dirt may form a black or gray deposit around the folds at the top of the canal. A brown or reddish-brown, waxy-looking substance in the ear-canal almost always indicates an ear infection.

Nose: It should be black and smooth. Whether it is moist or dry has little to do with the dog's temperature.

Gums: Should be a bright, clear pink. Some are partially pigmented. Puppies' gums may be slightly paler.

Tongue: Bright pink and clean. Spots or areas of pigment are normal.

Stool: The stool should be well formed. Slight diarrhea may be treated with a kaolin mixture; but frequent, watery eliminations or signs of blood or mucous, or a repulsive odor, indicate trouble.

Eating, drinking and toilet habits vary with the individual, but significant changes in any of these areas are grounds for suspecting trouble.

A dog's tongue is one clue to his state of health. The healthy dog's tongue will be bright pink and clear—spots or areas of pigment are normal.

BEWARE OF ACCIDENTAL POISONING

OUTDOOR living is fun for dog and master but summertime activities can put hazards in the path of an inquiring pet.

Gardening, painting, warfare against insects and rodents, and backyard barbecues are possible sources of canine poisoning.

Barbecues themselves, of course, are harmless. But the aluminum foil in which food is often broiled can choke him or lodge in his intestines. Don't leave foil, coated with meat drippings, where the dog can get at it. He'll probably try to chew the foil and, most likely, swallow some.

Place waste food in tightly closed, animal-proof garbage pails. Don't let perishable dog foods sit around too long in hot weather. They can cause severe intestinal upsets if eaten after they've begun to spoil.

Try to keep the dog away from areas treated with pesticides and don't spray places where the dog runs. Most of these products contain dangerous poisons.

Sometimes even inhaling pesticide fumes over a long period builds up toxicity and may eventually cause serious illness or death.

Lead poisoning is another canine killer. Don't use lead-base paint on dog houses, sleeping boxes, or any surface a dog might be tempted to chew. Keep the dog away from surfaces freshly covered with lead-base paints. If paint smears on his coat, he might be poisoned trying to lick it off.

All paints, insecticides, rodent poisons, turpentine, disinfectants, and similar products should be stored where the dog cannot come in accidental contact with them.

Secondary poisoning usually occurs when the dog eats a rodent that has died from poisoned bait. Most rodent poisons are particularly lethal and don't lose potency. They'll poison another animal as effectively as they did the creature for which they were intended.

If you set out poisoned bait, be sure it's where the dog can't sample it or a rat can't drag it into the open. Also check the dog's run frequently to make sure a poisoned rodent hasn't wandered into it, then died.

Nausea, trembling and pain are the most common early symptoms of poisoning. The owner's first step is to call a veterinarian and follow his advice. However, fast treatment is essential. Owners should have emetic and antidote on hand to use when immediate veterinary assistance is not available. When poisoning is suspected, first make the dog vomit, then administer the antidote. Equal parts of hydrogen peroxide and water, or a strong salt or dry mustard and water solution, induce nausea. When the dog has cleared his stomach, give activated charcoal for an antidote in recommended dosages for his weight and size. All supplies are available from any drugstore.

These steps are emergency first aid. Veterinary attention should be given the dog as soon as possible. The owner should note symptoms, as well as the possible cause of poisoning, for accurate diagnosis and treatment.

Supervised exercise is the best of all accident preventatives. The dog on a leash, safely confined in a fenced yard, or walking with his master, has little opportunity to find poisons or trouble of any kind.

DOGS IN WINTERTIME

THE WORST thing to do to a dog in winter is to put him by a radiator and leave him there until spring. The dry air will ruin his coat and the heat will make him lazy and listless when he ought to be exercising. Indeed, a dog needs more exercise in winter than he does in summer. He also requires more food, including some oil in his diet, to insure a beautiful coat; this is due to the fact that there is less humidity in winter. If he's getting a regular diet of a good commercial dog food, you needn't worry about the oil; just be sure he gets as much food as he needs.

Some people make the mistake of thinking that

dogs, like bears, should hibernate when December rolls around. Many also think it's wrong to wrap a sweater around a dog in winter. Nothing could be further from the truth. No dog, and particularly shorthairs, should be exposed to severe cold without some kind of cover. By severe cold we mean temperatures well below the freezing point.

Not only are sweaters essential, so are boots. Hunting dogs are generally preconditioned against the hazards of winter underfoot, but not the average home-dog. That's why you notice your dog limping or stopping short when he's walking on snow or ice. The snow burns his pads and gets between his toes, where it burns some more. Even worse than the snow and ice is the salt that is spread to melt the ice. A dog that is not used to snow and is going to be in it for any appreciable amount of time should be dressed in boots (available at most pet-supply stores). Failing boots, the pads should be washed in warm water to get rid of any salt, and dried carefully and thoroughly. Where there hasn't been any exposure to salt, it's enough to wipe the feet and dry them well.

No dog, including a Siberian Husky, should be exposed suddenly to very cold air. That is, you should never take a dog from the side of a radiator or fireplace, where the temperature is probably near 80, and rush him into freezing or sub-freezing out-of-doors. No dog—again including the Siberian Husky breed —can take such a change without getting sick, possibly seriously. Dogs are subject to just about all the winter ailments that affect humans, including pneumonia.

Unless the weather is too severe, dogs should be exercised every day in winter. If they can't be run, they should be walked at a good pace. If there is snow on the ground, be sure to keep them on leash. They love to run in snow and have a very bad habit of running into plowed roadways. Many dogs have been killed by cars on such roadways, because they were let off the leash.

Young puppies and very old dogs should never be taken out into severe cold. Old dogs should never be kept out too long. If you notice a sniffle or a runny nose, a cough or raspy breathing, don't lose time getting to your veterinarian. The dog could come down with a serious illness. In this regard, it's not a good idea to bathe a dog in winter. If he's so dirty that you can't stand it, give him a good brushing. If that doesn't do the job, try a dry shampoo. *Never place a wet dog in a draft.*

Where does your dog sleep in winter? His bed should be free of any drafts, off the floor, and away from direct heat, such as radiator or stove. He should have plenty of rugs or blankets, so that he can snuggle to his heart's content.

If your dog sleeps outside, his house should be checked against any cracks or holes. Make sure his bedding is off the ground. The floor should be well insulated and topped with straw or old carpeting or rug and there should be plenty of blankets.

Young puppies and very old dogs should never be taken out into severe cold.

PROBLEMS OF OLD AGE

SYMPTOMS of old age begin at different times in different dogs. This "individual difference" may be due to the dog's breeding, diet, environment, life style, and general health. No one can tell how long a dog is going to stay fit or how long it's going to live. There are some general "rules of thumb" that can help the dog owner estimate the longevity of his dog. The larger breeds generally have a shorter life span than the smaller breeds. This seems to be due to their tend-ency to "burn themselves out" more rapidly. It seems that a dog ages approximately seven "years" in one calendar year. Thus at five years of age a dog is roughly equivalent to a 35-year-old human. It shouldn't be surprising, therefore, to find six-year-old dogs with the typical problems of a middle aged man —cardio vascular disease, kidney disease, and digestive disturbances.

With the advent of modern medical therapy, the

Symptoms of heart disease in a dog include coughing, excessive tiring and fainting.

life span of your dog can also be extended. Problems which in past years were untreatable and could be solved only with euthanasia are today being medicated. Regular yearly check-ups can make early diagnosis and treatment possible, thus hopefully guaranteeing a longer and healthier life for your pet.

Kidney Disease

The most frequent affliction of the older dog is chronic kidney disease. Most deaths of older dogs are caused by this condition. The symptoms are increased thirst and urination, loss of appetite, and weakness. The diagnosis can be made by laboratory tests and prompt treatment may save the dog.

Heart Disease

Symptoms of this condition are coughing, excessive tiring, and fainting. If the disease is allowed to advance, it will lead to congestive heart failure signaled by fluid in the abdomen and swelling of the limbs. Your veterinarian can treat cardio-vascular disease with drugs, as well as recommending special diets and limited exercise.

Dental Problems

The older dog is often beset by loose or infected teeth; these should be extracted. This condition is due to natural aging as well as neglect. All dogs should have regular dental check-ups. Tartar should be removed before it is allowed to damage tooth enamel and gums. Periodic brushing of the teeth with salt and soda is recommended. Hard dog biscuits are also helpful in maintaining sound oral hygiene. If a dental problem is present, hard items should be avoided.

Diet

If your older dog is not displaying any digestive difficulties or gaining excess weight, then the regular maintenance diet can be continued. However, constipation and poor appetite often plague the older pet. Your veterinarian can prescribe a special diet to alleviate some of these problems.

Signs of Aging

At about six to seven years of age the dog's beard will probably begin to gray. Typically, then, the eyes begin to fail, followed by the hearing and finally the heart.

Whether to have your vet put the dog to sleep should only become a concern if the dog is suffering or if it becomes a real burden. Some dogs live to be 13 years or older, age gracefully, and then die peacefully and naturally. This will undoubtedly be a most painful loss, and in all probability the only grief that dog ownership will bring you.

The End

The question of disposing of the remains does arise. Some people have their veterinarian handle this task, other with strong emotional ties are desirous of a lasting memento. This need seems to have created a new commercial endeavor—the pet cemetery and pet coffins.   We know a family that is very active in the dog fancy—owns perhaps up to 40 dogs at one time, shows, breeds, grooms, etc.—and they have their favorite buried in the back yard under a special marker. Time will tell how you personally wish to handle this delicate matter.

What Next?

To ease the inevitable loss, consider getting another dog—perhaps a puppy—to keep your senior citizen company during his declining years. Frequently a young playmate instills new vim into an older pet and you may see frolicking and playing like never before. Avoid jealousy by still letting the older one have his own possessions, special spot and your love and attention. If you handle this successfully the results can be fantastic; your dog has a companion and when old age finally takes its toll you are not totally alone. The other solution is to adopt another dog after your pet departs. However, the difficulty is that finding the right one is often not so easy or so quick and with a saddened heart you may not be as discriminating and objective as you would wish. In any case, do get another dog! Don't believe that because of the grief just suffered that you won't do it again! Nonsense! If you've enjoyed dog ownership and all its rewarding experiences then by all means start anew. The next endeavor may be even more satisfying and enjoyable.

HOW MUCH TO FEED YOUR DOG?

Of the 27 million dogs in our country the chances are that more are overfed than are underfed. If the dog experts are right, it is an even bet that the underfed one is the healthier because he has to scrounge around for his sustenance and that exercise is good for him. Conversely the "fat boy" is more apt to be pampered to an earlier demise.

A good rule of thumb to follow in determining the condition of a dog is to keep him fat enough so that his ribs can be felt—but not so thin that they can be seen.

FIRST AID CHART

Condition	First Aid	Treatment
Burns	Use wet packs of cold water or ice cold water.	Consult your vet.
Choking	If possible remove foreign body from mouth or throat.	If not possible, consult your vet.
Diarrhea	When due to dietary changes, administer kaopectate according to dog's size.	If this continues, consult your vet.
Fits or Convulsions	Keep animal warm and quiet. If very wild try to prevent injury to self.	Consult vet.
Cuts	Minor cuts are licked clean by the dog. Wounds should be washed thoroughly and antiseptic and bandage should be applied if necessary.	Deep cuts should be stitched.
Dog Bites	Allow dog to lick them clean. If deep, wash them.	Deep bites should be stitched.
Fractures	Handle the dog carefully and muzzle him. Keep him warm and rush him to vet.	X-ray and setting of fracture are handled by vet.
Heatstroke	Due to excessive exposure to heat, dog displays panting, collapse, and fever. Place animal in cool area—administer wet packs to body.	Rush to vet for treatment.
Motion Sickness	Remove from moving vehicle. Allow stomach to settle before feeding.	Future trips should be pre-planned with anti-motion sickness medication.
Poisoning	Check container for correct antidote—administer immediately.	Rush to vet.
Porcupine Quills	Muzzle dog. Tie-clip ends of quills, then remove with pliers. Remove those near eyes and mouth first.	Vet may continue under anesthesia.
Shock	Caused by severe injury or illness. Keep animal warm and quiet. Cover with blankets.	Rush to vet.
Snake Bites	Cut X-shaped mark over fang print with sharp knife. Apply tourniquet between body and wound—suction out poison.	Rush to vet for anti-venom.
Stings (Insect)	Apply a paste of bicarbonate of soda or a weak solution of ammonia.	

Antidotes for Common Poisons

Cause vomiting—administer a mixture of half peroxide and water.

Poison	Source	Antidote
Acids	Batteries, etc.	Bicarbonate of soda
Alkali	Drain cleaners, etc.	Vinegar
Arsenic	Spray materials, etc.	Epsom salts
Food poisoning	Spoiled food, Garbage	Peroxide followed by epsom salts and a warm water enema
Lead	Paint	Epsom salts followed by milk
Mercury	Broken thermometer	Egg white and milk
Phosphorus	Rat poison	Peroxide
Sedatives	Medication	Strong coffee
Thallium	Insect poison	Table salt

First Aid—Restraint

Before you begin to administer first aid of any kind to an injured dog protect yourself by either muzzling the dog or by applying a self-made restraint. To make a restraint use anything readily available—a necktie or piece of rope—and loop it around the dog's mouth; tie above and then below and then bring up behind the ears and knot.

Safety Tips

Leashing
Many people still believe a dog is only happy when he is free to roam. They fail to realize that a dog is a remarkably adaptable creature and is far happier and safer when exercised in his own securely fenced yard or on a leash. To let your dog run loose, risking death or painful injury under the wheels of a fast-moving car, is downright cruelty.

Poison Prevention
Most dog poisoning isn't perpetrated by fiends. Careless dog owners are the culprits. Puppies especially will taste practically anything—paint, turpentine, insecticides, weedkillers, household bleaches and detergents. These common household supplies should be stored out of a curious pup's reach. After using insect sprays and fertilizers on your lawn, take care so that your dog doesn't get them on his feet and lick them off. When you suspect your dog has been poisoned, consult the veterinarian for emergency first aid treatment. Take him to the doctor as soon as possible.

Avoid Eye Injuries
When your dog rides with his head out the car window, he is in danger of incurring eye and ear injuries. Bits of grit blown with the force of a bullet into tender eye and ear tissues can start a painful infection.

Travel Notes
When traveling with your pet, always snap on his leash before you open the car door. An excited unleashed dog may dash headlong into traffic or scamper off to explore the countryside and get lost. In hot weather never leave your pet in a tightly closed car. Automobile interiors heat up rapidly, and dogs are very susceptible to heat prostration.

Dangerous Toys
Many dogs treasure a rubber bone or ball for years; others will chew them and swallow the pieces. If your dog attacks his toys like Jack the Ripper, avoid those made with metal rivets, staples or other materials he can tear apart and swallow. Many good, safe toys are available, so choose your dog's playthings carefully.

BREEDING/PREGNANCY/PUPPIES

SHOULD YOU BREED YOUR DOG?

FOR the professional breeder, this is primarily a question of genetics. For the non-professional, it is also a personal question of whether you want the additional work, excitement, and involvement that goes with breeding: 1) finding a suitable stud, 2) mating the dogs, 3) special care for the pregnant female, 4) staying at home around the time of birth, 5) helping care for the puppies, and 6) selling the puppies. The financial aspect must also be considered. Sometimes there are stud fees, vet fees, and then no living puppies.

Nevertheless, breeding can be a most enjoyable and rewarding experience. The difficulties encountered before the birth of the puppies are forgotten when the joys of watching cuddly pups frolic, eat, and sleep begin. Also, watching your female suddenly and naturally become a fine mother is a heartwarming experience. The children can become involved with the care of the puppies if you want to make this a family project.

An important factor to consider is the timing of the birth of the litter. There are many responsibilities involved in the birth and care of the litter—indicating that much time and energy is needed in order to provide proper care. Keep in mind that the gestation period is from 60 to 63 days. After the birth, the mother usually takes good care of her puppies, but supervision is needed to make sure all the pups are healthy, eating well and resting enough. Once the pups are weaned, they must be fed several times a day and soiled newspapers must be changed often.

If the litter is more than two puppies, small whelping quarters are soon outgrown. Large breeds grow very rapidly and if they aren't sold by eight weeks, they need a sizeable area. Some novice breeders have had to give away fine dogs because they didn't have enough room to keep them until they could be sold.

Before you even consider whether you have the time, money, space, and patience to start breeding, the genetic qualities of your bitch must be honestly evaluated. If she has serious faults, it would be best not to breed her, as these faults would be genetically carried on to her young. If she has no basic faults and is a healthy dog with a pleasant temperament, breeding can be considered.

There is work, planning, cost, and effort involved if the job is going to be done correctly. If the true love of dogs and wishing to further the improvement of the breed isn't your main goal, then you really shouldn't go into it. For the amateur, there is usually little, if any, profit to be made. Most amateur breeders consider this their hobby and operate at a loss. To become a professional requires extensive experience and a sizeable investment in order to have quality breeding stock and the adequate facilities of a true business venture.

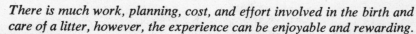

There is much work, planning, cost, and effort involved in the birth and care of a litter, however, the experience can be enjoyable and rewarding.

THE BREEDING PROCESS

Selecting the Male

UNLESS you are actively involved in the dog world, you may not know a good stud for your bitch. You can get help from your vet, from the breeder who sold you your dog, or from your local or national specialty breed organization. You should be able to get advice on whether to line breed, outcross, or possibly inbreed.

Inbreeding—This is the mating of very close relatives—father to daughter, brother to sister, mother to son. The novice or amateur breeder should not attempt this type of breeding. Inbreeding accentuates faults and is *not a good practice.*

Linebreeding—This is the mating of more distant relatives. Close linebreeding results in more predictable traits in the puppies.

Outcrossing—This is the mating of previously unrelated dogs of the same breed. Breeders usually use this method when they want to correct a fault or when they want to introduce another strain.

It is important to keep your breeding purposes in mind. Are you trying to get better hunting dogs, better show dogs, or dogs with fine temperament for children? Different purposes should result in a different selection of your stud.

This is just a very brief discussion of a complex subject. Those readers who wish to work on improving the breed should do a great deal of research in genetics and study what previous research findings have revealed. Breeding dogs can be most rewarding if done properly. Disappointments and needless expensive mistakes can be avoided by a careful approach.

The Stud

Locating a good stud dog for your bitch is of vital importance. Where you live can influence how difficult this may be. Sometimes if there isn't a quality stud available in your locale, the bitch must be transported to the stud, by rail or air.

Finding the stud can be accomplished by talking to people knowledgeable about dogs—such as breeders, handlers, your vet. All the investigating must be done prior to the time of your bitch's heat.

Once the stud has been selected, arrangements for the mating should be made. The best time to bring the bitch will be decided by her heat cycle. There is now a simple fertility test where Tes-tape is used to determine whether the bitch has ovulated. Many stud owners like to have the bitch arrive a day or so before the actual mating so that she can relax and be more at ease. Often they will keep a bitch for a few days so that the mating can be repeated. The details as to when to bring her to the stud, and how long to leave her, should be worked out in advance.

Stud Fee

The financial arrangement with the stud's owner should be discussed prior to the time of mating. Some stud owners prefer to be paid a set fee for this service, and they will usually give a repeat service if no living puppies result. Other stud owners ask for one or even two puppies, and they will usually specify that they want the "pick of the litter." Champion studs (those dogs that are already champions) usually get a higher fee than non-champions. Supply and demand also affect the fee. Some studs will only be bred to "approved bitches." That is, if the stud's owner doesn't feel the bitch is fine enough to breed, stud service won't be given.

Stud Service Certificate
(SIGNED GUARANTEE OF MATING)

This is to certify that: Certificate No._____

THE BITCH *MAR-ELS CREAM PUFF*

Breed *WEST HIGHLAND TERRIER* Registration No. *R-441969*

Owned by *Mrs. Susan K. Bernstein*

Address _____ *Glenese, Ill.*

Was bred to my STUD DOG *Ch. WIG MAC NAME SAKE* Reg. No. *R-223875*

Date bred *DEC 9-10-11* 19 *68* Due to whelp *FEB 9-10 11* 19 *69*

Cash Fee $_____ Received Full Paym't $ *100.00* Rec'd PART paym't $_____

Additional Conditions:_____

_____

CONDITIONS OF SERVICE (and a part of this contract)

No fee refunded in whole or in part.
A guarantee of actual mating (and "tie") only is made and not of pregnancy or of puppies living or dead.
If bitch fails to be in whelp (pregnancy), the owner must give notice to me not later than fifty days after date of mating. A RETURN SERVICE will be given to the same stud without charge, at the next heat (and only this next heat). If there is no pregnancy, owner of bitch to pay all expense and shipping charges both ways. Unless such notice is given, the right to a return service is forfeited.
If my stud dies, is sold, or otherwise not available, I have the right to mate the bitch with one of my other studs, my choice, unless both parties agree mutually on another choice.
If bitch changes ownership, right of full return service is at my option.
In order to assure myself of the pregnancy condition of the bitch, the right to see and examine her is granted.
If puppy is to be received instead of cash fee, I will

make my choice of litter—at age of 8 weeks. One puppy constitute a litter and if there is only one puppy, regardless of sex, this puppy shall constitute my choice of litter.
If all puppies are born dead, or none survive to age of 8 weeks, I have the postponed right to choice of puppy thru mating at next heat to my stud, but a repeat service is at my option. NO cash compensation is due me. If same condition occurs at second whelping, obligations of both parties are terminated. These rights (choice of puppy) are not affected by change of ownership of bitch.
It is specifically agreed hereby that the owner of the stud is not obligated to sign application for registration of this litter until and unless the stud fee has been paid in full (or, in case of puppy fee, the stud owner has gotten possession of puppy or puppies as agreed).
Important — Any ADDITIONAL or SPECIAL AGREEMENTS, conditions or provisions are noted on the other side of this certificate, over my written signature.

Signed *Mrs. E. K. Fischer*
_____ Owner of stud dog

Signed *Mrs. Susan Bernstein*
_____ Owner of bitch

This form is the property of and is sold by DOG WORLD MAGAZINE, 469 E. Ohio St., Chicago 11. It must not be copied or imitated in any way.

The Female—In Heat

Scientifically, the reproductive period is called the "estrus cycle" or the "heat period" or "in season." A female puppy will "come into heat" after six months of age. Some breeds, usually large ones, may be older. After the first heat, the others will follow at fairly regular six-month intervals. Illness and change of climate can alter this regularity. The first indication of the beginning of the heat period is a swelling of the external genitalia. This is followed in a few days by a slightly pinkish, liquidy discharge which gradually becomes a darker red in color. Some dogs are very meticulous, and you will barely be able to observe any discharge. Others are not so neat, and great care must be taken so they do not soil carpets and furniture. This bloody discharge continues from about a week to ten days. There are "sanitary belts" for dogs on the market if you should find this necessary. When the discharge begins to diminish, the female is ready for mating. She may be receptive for approximately two to 14 days. If you do not plan to mate your dog, *extreme* care must be used to prevent any accidental encounters. The urine of a female in heat has an odor which is very attractive to all male dogs. Their appearance on your doorstep may well be your first indication that your female is in heat. Many people board their female in a kennel for the duration of this period. Others drive their female some distance from the house so she can urinate without attracting all the neighborhood males to the house. The female in heat must never be left out alone. Even a fenced yard is not safe.

There are some products available which claim to remove this "odor" from the female in season. However, none of them seem to be 100 per cent effective.

Actually, the female is happiest when able to be home with you during this time. So, if you can exercise care that no unplanned meetings occur, heat is really no problem. Often the puppy's first heat is quite distressing to her. She may have cramps and feel very uncomfortable. Affection and understanding will help her to be more at ease during this time. While in "heat," your female will ask to go out quite frequently. She will be somewhat anxious and may not be in the mood to play or frolic. Her appetite might increase. Such behavior is temporary and quite normal.

During her "heat period" the female is usually happiest when able to remain at home. Great care must be taken to prevent accidental matings.

Mating the Female

Accidental

If an unplanned mating does occur, your vet can be of great assistance. Raising mongrel puppies is expensive and unnecessary! Your vet can give the female an injection which will end the pregnancy and will, in no way, prevent her from having future litters.

Planned

Should you intend to breed your female, planning must be done well in advance. Most dog authorities recommend not breeding at the first heat. Thus, the approximate date of ensuing heats should be calculated after the first.

The reproductive capacity of the female diminishes after age five, and, in many breeds, the reproductive cycle ends by age eight. However, there are great individual differences, and there have been numerous reports of bitches having litters well past this age.

Spaying

When puppies are not desired at any time, it is usually advisable to spay the female. This is an operation performed by the veterinarian which involves the removal of the ovaries. Today, when carried out in a modern animal hospital, this is a relatively safe operation. It is generally agreed that the best time for this procedure is after the dog has reached its full growth and not before. Spaying should, in no way, affect the dog's temperament or personality. It was once believed that dogs that had been spayed would become excessively fat. However, it has been found that this obesity is due to overfeeding and lack of exercise.

Bitches that have been spayed have a lower incidence of cancer of the reproductive system. Thus, this is a real advantage to the procedure. The "heat cycle" ceases, and the dog is safe from future pregnancies. Since this operation is irreversible, the female can never have puppies.

The cost of this operation will vary in different areas of the country. The cost should be weighed in terms of the advantages and other savings—no boarding while in heat—no accidental pregnancies!

The Male

As the owner of a male, you may wonder if you should use your dog as a stud. It seems like a relatively easy and appealing idea. For just a little work you can get a fee or a puppy. However, there is usually more to it than what meets the eye. First of all, some owners of male dogs find that the dog's personality changes when he is used for stud. Stud dogs can become very independent, not as affectionate as they previously were, and they may desire to roam. Most dog owners who have a single male, primarily as a pet, do not use them for stud as a general practice. However, there are occasions when a fine male is used, and it doesn't seem to do any real harm.

The basic question is whether the dog is of such quality to warrant his use as a stud. The purposes of the mating should be kept in mind. If the male is an outstanding hunting dog or a champion in conformation or obedience, it seems only natural to wish to perpetuate his remarkable qualities. A dog used for stud should himself be well-bred; he should have a good temperament and a constructionally sound build.

The care of the stud dog is most important. He should receive at least one good meal per day, and, if working hard, he should receive two. The meal should be well-balanced and high in protein. Ample exercise to keep him physically fit is vital.

Most breeders feel that ten months is the youngest age at which to begin using a male dog as a stud. The first mating must be handled carefully so that the novice stud can be taught everything that is necessary. It is best to use an experienced bitch the first few times. Mating no more frequently than once a month until the age of two years is recommended. After the age of two, a healthy stud can be used once a week. However, if he shows signs of tiring or disinterest, he should be rested for longer periods.

The fee for stud service is based on the average fee being charged for a specific breed. A stud who is a proven sire and a champion will command a higher fee than a non-champion.

It is the responsibility of the owner of the stud dog to care for the bitch while she is in his kennel or home for the mating. This means providing sleeping quarters, food, and exercise, as well as strict protection from unplanned matings.

If the use of the stud is to be a "genuine business enterprise," then he should probably be shown either for conformation, obedience, or field trials. Advertising in dog magazines would also be advisable.

All this work requires time, patience, and money. For the average dog owner, it is probably not the best idea. Even large kennels will often use other studs rather than maintaining their own.

The Mating

An experienced stud dog and an experienced brood bitch may need little assistance in mating, but, for the inexperienced, help is sometimes necessary.

The female will allow the male to mount her only when she is at the stage in her heat cycle when conception can occur. If she is watched carefully, this time is not too difficult to determine. She will become quite flirtatious and allow the male to make advances. It is considered advisable to repeat the mating twice. This repetition seems to give a better guarantee of conception. Although each female is different, noted dog authorities recommend breeding the 13th day and on alternate days until she again refuses.

The mating process itself should be handled slowly and carefully, allowing the bitch and stud to get acquainted in a controlled environment at first so that no fights can occur. Once they have familiarized themselves and seem interested, they can be allowed to come together. If the bitch is very nervous and aggressive, it is wise to use a muzzle so that she won't bite the male.

In the normal progression of mating, the male will mount the female and after the penis penetrates the bitch, the dogs will become "tied." This "tie" may last from just a few minutes up to an hour. Although a long-lasting tie is not necessary for conception, it is wise for the breeder to try to keep the dogs together for at least five minutes.

If there is a significant difference in size between the male and female, they may need special assistance. A male that is small may need a platform on which to stand and toy breeds are most easily mated on a table.

On occasion, the female will take a distinct dislike to a particular stud and not allow him to approach her. In such a case, it is wise, if possible, to use another stud.

Another problem is that sometimes the stud is not able at first to penetrate a willing female. It is best to separate them. Give the stud a rest of an hour or two and then, with much encouragement, let him try again. Never allow the stud to tire himself excessively in unsuccessful attempts.

After a mating, both dogs should be allowed to rest. Therefore, it is best not to rush the female home immediately after mating.

PREGNANCY

Care of the Expectant Mother

THE normal length of gestation (pregnancy) is 63 days. However, puppies can be healthy if born a few days earlier or later.

The care of the prospective mother is most important. She should be free of internal and external parasites. Worming should be done before the mating. She should be well fed but not overweight. During the first few weeks, she can have her regular diet, which can be supplemented with extra protein foods and vitamins. After the fifth week, she should be allowed additional food; however, she should not be allowed to get fat, as this will make her delivery very difficult. Cooked eggs, milk, and meat, in addition to a well-balanced commercial dog food, will give her the extra protein that she needs.

Plenty of exercise in the form of walking is best. Toward the end of her pregnancy, she should have several short walks rather than one overly long one. Undue stress and excitement should be avoided. Jumping and climbing stairs should not be allowed the last few days prior to whelping. She should be kept clean and well-groomed. The breast area should be clipped if necessary and any discharge from the vulva should be washed regularly.

False Pregnancy

False pregnancy can occur with or without a mating. The bitch develops all the signs of pregnancy—swollen nipples, enlarged abdomen, increased appetite—and yet she has not conceived.

Reabsorption

Sometimes a bitch will be pregnant and then, for some still unknown reason, will reabsorb the puppies.

Signs of Pregnancy

During the first few weeks, it is quite impossible to tell if the bitch is pregnant. After the fifth week, there is often an enlargement of the nipples. Then, after the sixth week, there may be a visible widening of the abdominal area. At this time, your vet can usually confirm the pregnancy.

WHELPING

FOR the novice breeder, this is a most exciting and somewhat frightening event, but, with proper planning and a clear understanding of what will and can occur, it need not be overwhelming.

It would probably be wise to take your dog to the vet to confirm the pregnancy. This confirmation is usually not possible until she is in the sixth week. Therefore, most authorities suggest that a high protein diet, vitamins, and exercise be administered from the breeding until delivery. When you visit the vet, he will check her to make sure she is in good health, and this is also a good time to ask for any suggestions that he may have for the whelping. If the bitch is very hairy, he may clip some of her hair around the nipples and the vulva area.

At least ten days before the due date, all the equipment for the whelping should be gathered. A *whelping box* of adequate size for the mother and pups should be placed in a warm and quiet place. Be certain it is large enough and that the sides are high enough to keep the puppies in, and that the mother can come and go comfortably. *Newspapers* should be saved, as they will be used in large amounts. Sterile *scissors, thread, rectal thermometer, hot water bottle, small towel-lined box* for the puppies, and clean *turkish towels* should all be readied.

To determine quite reliably when the puppies will arrive, check the bitch's temperature rectally at the same time at least once every day, beginning a week before she is due. Preferably, this can be done twice

WHELPING CALENDAR

Locate the date your bitch was bred in the left-hand column and the expected whelping date is in the right-hand column.

Date bred	Date due to whelp	Date bred	Date due to whelp	Date bred	Date due to whelp	Date bred	Date due to whelp	Date bred	Date due to whelp	Date bred	Date due to whelp	Date bred	Date due to whelp	Date bred	Date due to whelp	Date bred	Date due to whelp	Date bred	Date due to whelp	Date bred	Date due to whelp	Date bred	Date due to whelp
January	March	February	April	March	May	April	June	May	July	June	August	July	September	August	October	September	November	October	December	November	January	December	February
1	5	1	5	1	3	1	3	1	3	1	3	1	2	1	3	1	3	1	3	1	3	1	2
2	6	2	6	2	4	2	4	2	4	2	4	2	3	2	4	2	4	2	4	2	4	2	3
3	7	3	7	3	5	3	5	3	5	3	5	3	4	3	5	3	5	3	5	3	5	3	4
4	8	4	8	4	6	4	6	4	6	4	6	4	5	4	6	4	6	4	6	4	6	4	5
5	9	5	9	5	7	5	7	5	7	5	7	5	6	5	7	5	7	5	7	5	7	5	6
6	10	6	10	6	8	6	8	6	8	6	8	6	7	6	8	6	8	6	8	6	8	6	7
7	11	7	11	7	9	7	9	7	9	7	9	7	8	7	9	7	9	7	9	7	9	7	8
8	12	8	12	8	10	8	10	8	10	8	10	8	9	8	10	8	10	8	10	8	10	8	9
9	13	9	13	9	11	9	11	9	11	9	11	9	10	9	11	9	11	9	11	9	11	9	10
10	14	10	14	10	12	10	12	10	12	10	12	10	11	10	12	10	12	10	12	10	12	10	11
11	15	11	15	11	13	11	13	11	13	11	13	11	12	11	13	11	13	11	13	11	13	11	12
12	16	12	16	12	14	12	14	12	14	12	14	12	13	12	14	12	14	12	14	12	14	12	13
13	17	13	17	13	15	13	15	13	15	13	15	13	14	13	15	13	15	13	15	13	15	13	14
14	18	14	18	14	16	14	16	14	16	14	16	14	15	14	16	14	16	14	16	14	16	14	15
15	19	15	19	15	17	15	17	15	17	15	17	15	16	15	17	15	17	15	17	15	17	15	16
16	20	16	20	16	18	16	18	16	18	16	18	16	17	16	18	16	18	16	18	16	18	16	17
17	21	17	21	17	19	17	19	17	19	17	19	17	18	17	19	17	19	17	19	17	19	17	18
18	22	18	22	18	20	18	20	18	20	18	20	18	19	18	20	18	20	18	20	18	20	18	19
19	23	19	23	19	21	19	21	19	21	19	21	19	20	19	21	19	21	19	21	19	21	19	20
20	24	20	24	20	22	20	22	20	22	20	22	20	21	20	22	20	22	20	22	20	22	20	21
21	25	21	25	21	23	21	23	21	23	21	23	21	22	21	23	21	23	21	23	21	23	21	22
22	26	22	26	22	24	22	24	22	24	22	24	22	23	22	24	22	24	22	24	22	24	22	23
23	27	23	27	23	25	23	25	23	25	23	25	23	24	23	25	23	25	23	25	23	25	23	24
24	28	24	28	24	26	24	26	24	26	24	26	24	25	24	26	24	26	24	26	24	26	24	25
25	29	25	29	25	27	25	27	25	27	25	27	25	26	25	27	25	27	25	27	25	27	25	26
26	30	26	30	26	28	26	28	26	28	26	28	26	27	26	28	26	28	26	28	26	28	26	27
27	31	27	May 1	27	29	27	29	27	29	27	29	27	28	27	29	27	29	27	29	27	29	27	28
28	Apr. 1	28	2	28	30	28	30	28	30	28	29	28	29	28	30	28	30	28	30	28	30	28	Mar. 1
29	2			29	31	29	July 1	29	31	29	30	29	30	29	31	29	Dec. 1	29	31	29	31	29	2
30	3			30	June 1	30	2	30	Aug. 1	30	Sep. 1	30	Oct. 1	30	Nov. 1	30	2	30	Jan. 1	30	Feb. 1	30	3
31	4			31	2			31	2			31	2	31	2			31	2			31	4

Courtesy Gaines Dog Research Center.

Everything is in readiness for the whelping—the whelping bed, newspaper, scissors, alcohol, towels, and you to give moral support.

a day, morning and evening. Normal temperature is 101.2. The temperature will drop about twelve hours before whelping. When her temperature drops, place her in the whelping box and stay with her. As the whelping time comes closer, the bitch will probably do a great deal of nesting. She will tear the paper in her box or she may find another spot which she favors and start building a "nest." Encourage her to get accustomed to the box that you have provided and to sleep in it for several days before the big event.

When labor begins, stay with her constantly as she will need your encouragement. Since this is quite an emotional time for most dogs, it is best not to have any additional excitement; thus, limit the number of "visitors" into the delivery room. Try to keep as calm and quiet as possible. A puppy should be born about an hour after labor begins. Signs of labor differ between breeds and even between dogs in the same breed. Some bitches will whine and cry, and some will lie quietly, get up and scratch around and dig in their whelping box, and then suddenly push out a puppy without making a sound.

When a bitch strains hard for a long period of time without making any progress, there may be a problem. If nothing happens after one hour, call the vet and have him advise you. Don't wait too long—serious complications can result, such as the loss of pups and/or mother. The vet may want to see the bitch or he may tell you what to do. He may want to administer a shot to help things along or possibly a Caesarean section may be needed. This is a surgical procedure usually performed in a veterinary hospital. The bitch is given an anesthetic, and the pups are removed from the womb. This is necessary if the bitch is too small for normal delivery, if a pup is stuck in the

birth canal, or if the pup's head is too large. When such an operation is performed by a vet under proper conditions, it is not a dangerous operation. Usually the bitch can be taken right home afterwards and can nurse the puppies. Antibiotics to prevent infection are usually prescribed, which may be administered by injection or orally.

Some pups may arrive shortly after labor begins and others, with the vet's approval, may not be born for a day or two. The important factor is to have someone available to help her if necessary and to be certain that everything is going along correctly. Usually, a pup is born head first, but sometimes a pup may be breech—that is, come in another position rather than head first. Thus, the bitch may have difficulty, and you may have to assist her.

If part of the puppy is visible and yet keeps slipping back into the birth canal, then take hold of the puppy and pull gently in rhythm with each contraction. The membrane makes the pup wet and slippery so getting a firm hold may be quite difficult. Use a small piece of towel if you need a better grasp. Do not pull too hard or you may damage the pup.

As soon as the puppy is expelled, the membraneous sac in which it is enclosed should be torn open and removed and the umbilical cord cut. Then, the mother should lick the puppy clean and push it up to one of her teats to nurse. Again, you may have to assist here as some new mothers ignore their children. Quickly but gently dry and warm the puppy and place it by the mother to nurse.

After the whelping is finished, the mother is going to need a good cleaning. The breasts and bottom area should be washed with lukewarm water and mild soap, and then rinsed well. This will remove the discharges clinging to the mother from the delivery and will make for more sanitary conditions for her litter.

Reasons for a Caesarian Section

A puppy may be misplaced—sideways instead of head or feet first. It may be too large and thus be unable to move down the birth canal. On occasion, a puppy is dead, becomes stuck, and blocks the passage of the other puppies.

It is possible for a bitch to have more than one Caesarian operation. There are known cases of bitches having six such operations.

Assisting the Delivery

Surprisingly, instinct does not guide all bitches. Many are thoroughly confused as to what is happening to them and what they should be doing. It is not at all unusual for a bitch to expel a puppy and then to just sit there licking herself without doing her maternal job. The new mother *should* quickly tear open the sac which surrounds the puppy, bite off the um-

The new mother nursing her puppies—a healthy litter of four.

bilical cord and lick the puppy thoroughly to get it breathing and cleaned up. In your role as midwife be prepared to handle these matters if the mother neglects to do so. The most important thing is to quickly get the puppy out of the membrane sac in which it is enclosed at birth and to clear the lungs so that it can breathe. After removing the sac, cut the cord, rub the pup dry with a small turkish towel and hold it with its head downward and shake it gently. This should clear the lungs of fluid and help it to breathe. Too many puppy deaths have been attributed to respiratory failure which can be avoided. Fluid should be wiped off the puppy as it is expelled and the gentle downward shaking or swinging should be continued until no more fluid appears. Thoroughly drying the pup and keeping it warm is of utmost importance. The mother will probably eat the umbilical cord and the after birth which is perfectly natural and she should be allowed to do so as they seem to act as a laxative. If the litter is quite large it would be best to remove some of them so that she doesn't overdo a good thing. An afterbirth should be expelled after the delivery of each puppy. Any re-

maining within the uterus will cause infection and serious complications. Keep a paper and pencil near at hand to maintain an accurate record if the litter is large.

Frequently, there will be a little time between the births so that the new mother can rest and nurse her puppy. Once the straining of labor begins again, remove the puppies to the specially prepared puppy box close by. This is done in order to protect the pups from possible injury while the mother is giving birth. The box should be near enough, however, so that she can see and hear them for otherwise she may become needlessly concerned.

With the birth of each subsequent puppy the same procedure should be followed. If the mother is doing her part, don't interfere unless your services are needed. There may be times when a puppy is not breathing and the mother's licking and concern doesn't improve the situation. Take the puppy and rub it furiously with a towel to warm it and stimulate it. Shake it as described above. Continue working on it with rubbing and also proceed with mouth to mouth resuscitation. Open the pup's mouth and check for any obstruction.

Technique for Administering Mouth to Mouth Resuscitation

Put your mouth over the pup's nose and mouth and
(1) breathe into puppy's mouth

Yorkshire puppies and their mom on a most comfortable whelping bed. (Owned by Mrs. Dorothy Creeden.)

(2) inhale fresh air

(3) repeat.

Follow a regular breathing rhythm. Continue until breathing starts. Breathe gently as the puppies lungs are smaller.

When trouble arises it's so nice to have a veterinarian handy who can help you with: (1) oxygen—hold the oxygen mask over the pup's face for a few minutes (this is often quite successful), (2) an injection of adrenalin to stimulate respiration and the heart.

Difference of opinion exists as to how long it is wise to continue to attempt revival of a non-breathing pup. Some authors feel that it's never too late and to keep working vigorously until there is a response even if it takes hours. Most vets we queried felt that if the life processes didn't begin within a reasonable length of time after birth (approximately 15 minutes), even if the pup were revived, brain damage would have occurred. Since there is more to be gained from trying, it would be worthwhile to expend all the necessary time and energy to revive a "slow starting" puppy.

Most births are normal and follow a natural pattern. But one has to be prepared for any event. There are occasions when your bitch may expel an abnormal puppy. Remove it quickly so that the mother doesn't try to destroy it further or to eat it. When a bitch realizes that a pup is malformed or is going to die she may try to harm it. Sometimes bitches have been known to start this with one pup and then get hysterical and kill the entire litter. Such behavior is not usual but should be guarded against. If the bitch is highly agitated after the delivery and seems excessively rough with the pups—such as, biting them, ripping at their umbilical—then caution should be exercised. Separate her from the pups, if necessary, by putting them in their own heated, cozy box. Return them only for nursing every two hours until you see that the mother is acting normally. Consult your veterinarian—he may prescribe tranquilizers.

Usually during and after whelping, the bitch is quite tense, fearful, and overprotective of her new charges. Maintaining calm and quiet in her quarters at this time is highly recommended. Only family members should enter the nursery and they, too, should practice restraint. If the whelping box has been placed in a quiet and warm area, it is easy to maintain this necessary control. Veterinarians and breeders stress emphatically that for "preventative medicine" visitors should be kept from the "nursery" for several weeks. Infection spreads easily and avoiding unnecessary exposure is the wisest thing.

After you think the last pup has been born, consult with your veterinarian. He may wish to give the bitch an injection which would help to expel any matter still remaining in the uterus. Sometimes, there may even be another puppy.

Whelping is a strenuous experience for the bitch and she should get a tempting meal either between the delivery of pups or afterwards. She probably will not wish to leave her new charges so bring the food to her in the whelping box. Offer her some warm cereal with milk or cooked ground meat with broth —if she is reluctant to eat, coax her a little. Keeping her strength up at this point is most important for her and the nursing puppies. Allow her to go out to relieve herself. Probably it will be only for this purpose that she will leave her brood.

Compared to the human female the dog has a much quicker recuperation period. She is usually up and around all during whelping, running up and down stairs, immediately after and seemingly perfectly fit. Don't let this healthy appearance lull you into neglect. The postpartum period does have certain possible hazards. Beware of *eclampsia*—this is a type of convulsive paralysis which manifests itself by the dog shaking violently, its movement paralized, and high fever. Eclampsia is caused by a deficiency of blood calcium. Prompt administration of an injection of calcium gluconate should result in a remission of symptoms. Death can result if treatment is not initiated rapidly.

Peritonitis is an inflammation of the lining of the

abdomen that can result if the bitch does not completely expel everything from her uterus and birth canal. Signs of the existence of such a condition are: high fever and a greenish foul smelling vaginal discharge. Antibiotics may save the mother.

Mastitis is an infection of the breasts. It is another serious problem to be aware of. Should the breasts become red, swollen, hot and tender, immediate action is necessary. Puppies should not be allowed to nurse as the milk is infected and they will die. Pups should be hand fed and the mother seen and treated by the veterinarian.

PUPPIES

Hand Feeding Puppies

There are occasions when the hand feeding of puppies becomes necessary. The possible reasons may be death or sickness of the mother, insufficient milk because of the litter size, or neglect by the mother. When hand feeding is indicated, your job of caring for the puppies can become quite an ordeal. Here is the best procedure to follow:

(1) Use a fully prepared formula created for this purpose such as Borden's Esbilac.

(2) Feed it warmed. Keep unused portion refrigerated.

(3) There are several methods of feeding—a dropper, a small nipple and bottle made for puppies, or a stomach tube.

Once the technique of using the feeding tube is mastered, it is the fastest, easiest, and probably the most reliable method. The vet can teach you how to insert a feeding tube into the puppies' stomach and then to inject the required amount of formula into it with a syringe. In this manner, an entire litter can be fed in a short span of time and you can be certain of the amount ingested.

Using the dropper is a very slow process. The puppy must be held in an upright position and the milk is dripped onto the tongue and then swallowed. Great caution must be taken to prevent any liquid from getting into the lungs as this will result in pneumonia and death. There is also the fact that it is difficult to know how much milk the puppy has actually ingested as so much drips away. Using the scale before and after each feeding is the only way to know with certainty and this can become rather time consuming.

The nipple and bottle is also a slow feeding method which has the danger of allowing fluid to get into the lungs.

Since some controversy exists as to the frequency with which to feed puppies, your vet should be consulted. The amount to feed is determined by the size of the dog and he will advise you on this matter as well.

Be sure each puppy gets some colostrum from the mother. This is the watery looking substance which is the "first milk" that is so important in providing the pups with the vital immunities against infectious disease.

Post Whelping

After whelping, the bitch will have quite a copious blood-stained discharge for a week or two. This uterine discharge is normal and should stop after two weeks. The dam's temperature should return to normal at least forty-eight hours after whelping. If it is raised, an infection may exist and antibiotic treatment may be necessary.

Feeding the Bitch after Whelping

After delivery, the bitch will require a 50 to 100% increase in her normal food intake. For now, she must meet her own body needs as well as provide for her nursing puppies. Her diet should be rich in protein and provide ample liquid to help in the milk production. Eggs, meat, and milk can be added to enrich her diet. While she is nursing, she can be allowed to eat as much as she wants without fear of her becoming overweight.

Immediately after whelping, she may want her food brought to her in the whelping box—this should be done, because she is reluctant to leave her new litter. The first few days after whelping her diet can contain milk and milky preparations, such as cereal.

Often, bitches need to be coaxed to go out and relieve themselves during this time.

HOW TO TUBE FEED A PUPPY

Equipment

1. A 20 cc plastic disposable syringe.
2. One number eight infant feeding tube.
3. Prepared formula (Esbilac).

Have your veterinarian demonstrate the insertion of the tube the first time. At this time, mark the feeding tube to indicate the accurate depth of insertion necessary in order to place the formula into the stomach. Then, when feeding time arrives, attach the tube to the tip of the syringe and suck the warmed formula to fill the syringe with the required amount. Hold the puppy with one hand and gently insert the tube over the tongue and down into the stomach up to the mark on the tube. Very slowly, release the necessary amount of formula. Then, carefully withdraw the tube.

THE PUPPIES

WHAT a surprise you'll have the first time you behold a newborn puppy. It's all wet, tiny, and really doesn't look anything like the breed standard. Don't panic. Their features will change and develop as they mature, even the color of their fur will change. For example, Dalmatian puppies are born without their spots. Sometimes puppies will have areas where fur is not present at first. Don't be overly concerned about these minor findings. If the puppy is healthy and well-formed, then wait for time to remove some of these youthful blemishes. However, if the pup is malformed —and be sure this is so—then there is no sense in keeping it. At one time breeders would cut down the size of a litter by destroying those newborns who they felt were not "top" quality. Today, it is felt that a newly born puppy cannot be accurately evaluated. Sometimes the very one that you had intended to destroy may develop into a superior adult.

Weight

Weighing the pups at birth and then each day for the first week to ten days is good practice. By so doing, you can keep a close check on each pup and any that are not gaining sufficiently will come to your attention promptly. These should be allowed to nurse first so that the others don't put them aside. You may give them a supplemental bottle after each nursing period until they start to gain properly. Check with your vet as to the normal amount of weight gain desired for your breed. Use a baby scale for weighing the pups.

REVIEW OF PUPPY CARE

1. **Keep the babies warm and dry.**
2. **Watch their weight gain and, if necessary, give supplement feedings.**
3. **Keep the whelping box clean.**

"Crown Jewels Fiery Gold" very contented, looking over her new-born puppies just a few hours old. They are born white and at the age of three weeks, spots appear.

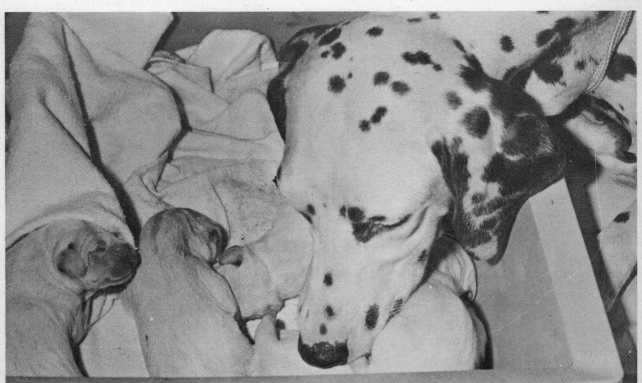

Temperature

Keeping the puppies warm is just as important as seeing that they are well-fed. The room should not only be warm, but also free from drafts. If the total room temperature cannot be maintained at 75 deg., then use well-protected heating pads. Take care that the cords are not exposed—dogs do have a tendency to chew on them. Another method of warming an area is to use a lamp. Place a room thermometer next to the whelping box so that you can be certain of the temperature in that spot.

Housekeeping

The whelping box itself should be kept dry and clean. After the births, remove all wet or soiled papers. The bottom of the box should be covered with several thick layers of newspaper. Some people like to stretch a towel across the bottom for extra warmth and softness. If you wish to do so, be sure to fasten it down well to prevent the pups from getting caught in or under it. The papers in the box should be changed as frequently as needed. For the first few weeks the mother usually is a terrific housekeeper. She will lick up any mess her children make. However, as they get older, this "clean-up patrol" will become your responsibility. If the nursery is not kept meticulously clean this becomes an invitation to infection and, needless to say, the odor can get rather overwhelming. Throw the soiled newspapers out of the house, otherwise your premises will rapidly develop a permeating reek.

Postnatal Care

After birth, most puppies are quite tired and may

CARING FOR HAND-FED OR ORPHANED PUPS

Normally the mother will lick her puppies in order to facilitate their urination and defecation. Should the puppies be orphaned—the mother ill or negligent—then this duty must be assumed. Gently wipe the anal area with a piece of moistened cotton until the puppy has a movement. With another clean piece of cotton, wipe the urinary area. This procedure should be followed before and after each feeding. It is essential to do this until the pups are mature enough to perform this bodily function independently.

---

want to sleep. If it has been an easy delivery, the pup may wish to nurse immediately. The mother will usually lick the new puppy from head to toe to clean it up and to get its circulation going. The mother also must lick the puppy in order to help it to urinate and defecate.

A healthy, strong puppy should be able to suck well and satisfy his needs, sucking quietly, stroking the mother as it sucks. The rear nipples have the most milk and puppies having difficulties in getting enough to eat should be placed there. If a puppy is still not getting enough milk from the mother, supplemental feeding may be necessary. Puppies are both blind and deaf at birth; they do not open their eyes until about the tenth day—some breeds are even slower.

Fading Puppies

This term is applied to puppies that are normal, healthy, and strong at birth, and then gradually sicken and die during the first week. The reason for this can be an infection in the puppies or in the mother which is being passed to the pups via the milk. That is why it is necessary to keep a close watch on the puppies and dam, to be certain that they are eating and growing—that they have fat, full tummies and are content. Sick puppies cry and crawl around aimlessly. Any signs of diarrhea should also be a warning. Contact your vet immediately if you see danger signals. Treatment immediately can often save you from needless loss. Supplementary feeding for a smaller pup is worthwhile.

Dew Claws, Tail Docking, and Ear Cropping

Your vet can remove your puppies dew claws. These are the "extra" nails slightly above the others, around ankle height. It is not necessary to remove them. However, they serve no useful purpose and just get in the way. This procedure is best done when the pup is four days old.

Many breeds require that their tails be docked for show purposes. This can be done at the same time as the removal of the dew claws. Again, since the docking should be done correctly, it should be handled by the vet.

A.K.C. Breeds Whose Tails Should Be Docked

Affenpinscher
Airedale
Australian Terrier
Bouvier des Flandres
Boxer
Brittany Spaniel
Brussels Griffon
Clumber Spaniel

Cocker Spaniel
Doberman Pinscher
Old English Sheepdog
English Toy Spaniel
Fox Terrier (smooth)
Fox Terrier (wire)
Toy Fox Terrier
German Shorthaired Pointer
German Wirehaired Pointer
Irish Terrier
Kerry Blue Terrier
Lakeland Terrier
Norwich Terrier
Pinscher (miniature)
Poodle (miniature)
Poodle (standard)
Poodle (toy)
Rottweiler
Schipperke
Schnauzer (giant)
Schnauzer (miniature)
Schnauzer (standard)
Sealyham Terrier
Silky Terrier
Springer Spaniel
Sussex Spaniel
Vizsla
Weimaraner
Welsch Corgi (pembroke)

Welsh Terrier
Wheaton Terrier

Some breeds should have their ears cropped. This operation should be conducted by a vet familiar with the breed standards. Cropping is usually done when the pups are eight weeks old. After surgery, the ears are taped and will heal by the time they are 12 weeks old.

A.K.C. Breeds Whose Ears Should be Cropped

Boston Terrier
Bouvier des Flandres
Boxer
Brussels Griffon
Doberman Pinscher
Great Dane
Manchester Terrier
Schnauzer (giant)
Schnauzer (miniature)
Schnauzer (standard)

Weaning

When the puppies are gradually taken off their mother's milk and given other food, this is called the weaning process. Depending on the breed and the size of the litter, weaning may take place between the age of three and six weeks.

Weaning can take piace when the puppies are between three and six weeks old. Once the pups start eating solid food, the mother will not clean up after them.

CAUSES OF PUPPY DEATHS

KEEPING a litter of newborn puppies alive can be a perplexing problem for dog-breeders. The problem may lie in a range of diseases of genetic, environmental, physiologic, or nutritional origin. However, it should be understood that the causes of most puppy losses have not been determined.

Investigators have observed the following general pattern: percentage of puppy losses was highest in young bitches, gradually diminished as the age of the bitch approached three years, then increased after four years; most mortalities occurred during the first week of life; high inbreeding increased neonatal mortality while hybrids of inbred breeds resulted in significantly reduced losses. In a comparison of male and female survival rates of more than 400 English Setter pups, there was little or no difference during the first week of life; however, at three and four weeks of age the male survival rate was slightly greater than female with 90.4% of the males and 89.5% of the females surviving.

The neonatal period, here arbitrarily defined as the first three weeks of life, is one in which puppies are physiologically immature. Selected normal physiological values are listed in Table 1. These illustrate the relatively undeveloped function of most physiological and behavioral activities of puppies during the first few weeks of life. Puppies also are immunologically immature although certain elements of the immune system have been shown to be functional prior to birth. Certain agents which are relatively innocuous to the mature dog are lethal to the newborn puppy.

Noninfectious Causes of Neonatal Puppy Death

While it is very difficult to determine the relative significance of various factors that cause death of newborn puppies during the first week of life, it appears that noninfectious disease conditions account for a large percentage of them. Fetal anomalies (congenital malformations), poor mothering, parasitism by round worms and hookworms, and, on rare occasions, neonatal *isoerythrolysis* are blamed.

Difficult or prolonged labor is a major cause of stillbirth, but it cannot be blamed for all nonviable puppies. The loss is estimated to be about 8%. Uterine inertia is a major cause. Contributing factors are excessive weight and lack of exercise, especially in certain small breeds. Obstruction of the birth canal also may contribute. This condition may result from old fractures or from fibrous bands across the vagina. Problems also may be caused by excessive puppy size, large heads of brachycephalic breeds, abnormal presentations, or fetal anomalies.

Because of the intense selection by many breeders for certain conformation characteristics, congenital abnormalities are becoming a more frequent cause of death of the newborn and now account for nearly 1% of newborn puppy deaths. They may be hereditary or may result from failure of the embryo to differentiate properly. Among the hereditary conditions, *chondrodystrophia fetalis* has been reported in Poodles, Scottish Terriers, and Fox Terriers. The fetus has a cretinous appearance with malformations of the limbs. *Congenital hydrocephalus* is not uncommon in the brachycephalic breeds and may be associated with malformation and doming of the cranium. *Congenital diaphragmatic hernia* has been reported to be hereditary, but it has been produced experimentally in pigs and rats by vitamin A deficiency. Cleft palate is considered to be a common hereditary cause of puppy death because of the inability of most affected puppies to suckle. Those puppies that do suckle have a high incidence of inhalation pneumonia. Harelip often is associated with cleft palate. Additional conditions have been described: congenital abnormalities of the lungs *(alveolar dysplasia);* failure of lungs to inflate *(primary atelectasis)* or a secondary atelectasis from inhalation of fluids at birth, *aplasia* of the kidneys; and occlusion of the anus, termed *atresia ani.* This condition produces a bloated pup that vomits sporadically and will cause death if not treated promptly.

Neonatal isoerythrolysis (neonatal hemolytic anemia) has occurred in A-positive pups born to A-negative mothers that had been immunized by previous transfusions of A-positive blood. As transfusion technology becomes more widely practiced, this condition may become more common. (It does not occur as a result of breeding dogs with incompatible blood groups.) Affected puppies become very pale within one to two days after birth; deaths usually occur within the first 72 hours. If puppies survive beyond this time, they usually do not die.

Poor mothering is one of the principal causes of neonatal deaths. A nervous, inexperienced bitch may cause trauma to her newborn puppies. Overzealous removal of fetal membranes may result in eviscera-

The percentage of puppy losses is highest with young bitches.

tion, umbilical herniation, and cannibalism. The provision of an adequate whelping box and close attention to the bitch are of greater value than administration of tranquilizing drugs. Starvation may result from the inability of puppies to suckle, as with premature or "runt" puppies, especially when they are weak or chilled. As mentioned above, developmental defects may reduce food intake or preclude it. Occasionally, a bitch will not settle long enough to allow puppies to suckle. Caked udder (edema) may make milk unavailable. Lack of milk, technically termed *agalactia,* has a number of causes: underdeveloped mammae; uterine infections; septicemia; mastitis due to staphylococci, streptococci, or mixed infections with coliform bacteria. A bitch with mastitis often will not allow puppies to suckle because of the pain.

Chilling accounts for many puppy deaths. A newborn puppy requires warmth, and an ambient temperature of at least 70°F should be provided during the first week of life if puppies are with the bitch. Thermoregulation is poor for the first eight days of age.

Newborn Puppy Deaths
Caused by Bacteria and Viruses

Bacterial Infections: Many cases of early death of puppies have been attributed to viral diseases; however, those that occur within the first few days of life, especially during the first 72 hours, usually have not been associated with any known virus. The principal viral cause of puppy losses, canine herpesvirus, affects primarily the one-to-three-week-old age group. It normally does not cause "fading pups." The clinical terms "acid milk syndrome," "toxic milk syndrome," and "puppy septicemia" have been ascribed to a variety of causes, usually bacterial. Although useful to the veterinarian or breeder in describing common clinical signs, the causes of these conditions are largely unknown. The "toxic milk syndrome" has been ascribed to incompatibility of neonatal puppies to bitch's milk. The puppies cry, become bloated, and have greenish diarrhea and red, swollen rectums. Most cases of "fading pups," however, are believed to be caused by bacterial infections. Affected puppies crawl away from the mother, or are disregarded, become chilled, cry, strain, and develop cyanosis. They become weak and die within 18 hours after birth, usually within a few hours after the first appearance of clinical signs. Temperatures are not elevated; they usually are subnormal. Often, a bitch will lose several litters in sequence. In such instances, litters of weak or stillborn puppies suggested the possibility of chronic uterine infection (metritis) in the bitch. This is a very insidious disorder whose clinical signs generally are not apparent to the owner. Bitches with a history of puppy losses should be examined carefully by a veterinarian for chronic metritis, endometritis, and vaginitis. If found to be infected, they should be treated intensively with systemic antibiotics at the time of estrum and at breeding. Treatment also should be given at or before the time of whelping to prevent infection of the newborn puppies. In general, during the first week of life, puppies from bitches that have suffered previous losses should be kept warm (80-85 F), given oral glucose, and treated with antibiotics. If the quality of the bitch's milk is questioned, puppies should be hand fed with a commercial formula such as Esbilac (Borden).

It should be emphasized that treatment is based on signs and general experience since the cause of puppy deaths is rarely determined.

The most common bacteria associated with neonatal pup deaths are streptococci and E. coli, with some losses reportedly caused by staphylococci and pseudomonas infections. Pseudomonas and E. coli infections have been associated with severe hemorrhagic enteritis whereas streptococci and staphylococci frequently are associated with umbilical infections. Brucella canis is associated with abortions after 45-55 days of gestation, stillbirths, early embryonic deaths, and occasional death of pups from infected bitches, but this organism is not a proven cause of neonatal puppy death.

Streptococcal infections (beta-hemolytic streptococci) are associated with puppies that are born vigorous and healthy, suckle well for the first 24 hours, then become suddenly weak and restless. They cry, show incoordination, develop tetanic spasms, and die. Affected puppies often are rejected by the bitch. All puppies in the litter may not die, and the bitch may not whelp infected litters subsequently. Affected puppies have peritonitis, a dark and enlarged liver, a blue-black and swollen umbilicus, and sometimes severe hemorrhagic enteritis. In such cases, streptococci may be isolated from the freshly obtained organs of dead puppies and from the vagina of the mothers. One author has shown transmission of beta-hemolytic streptococci within a kennel where several abortions occurred. He considers transmission from bitch to bitch by the male important. Also, carrier bitches have been identified.

Viral Infections: Although several viruses may infect puppies, only the canine herpesvirus has been associated with naturally occurring neonatal illness and death. Occasionally, pups may die from canine adenovirus infections (canine hepatitis virus) or distemper, but these have been reported only in laboratory studies. These studies have shown that both distemper and hepatitis viruses may infect embryos with resultant stillbirth or birth of weak pups that later die. The low incidence of neonatal mortality caused by these viruses may be one of the benefits of widespread vaccination preventing the spread of virulent virus. There are no reports that either attenuated distemper or hepatitis viral vaccines given to pregnant bitches have produced abortions or infections of the fetus. *From Cornell Research Laboratory for Diseases of Dogs.*

NORMAL PHYSIOLOGIC VALUES FOR YOUNG PUPPIES

Weight Gain	Two-fold increase per 8-10 days; about 1 gram per pound expected adult weight per day.
Body Temperature	Weeks 1-2: 94-99 F. Weeks 2-4: 97-100 F.
Water Requirement	2-3 oz/pound/day; turnover about 2 times that of adult.
Caloric Requirement	60-100 Kcal/pound/day. Newborn pups become hypoglycemic if not fed for 24 hours, especially toy breeds.
Respiratory Rate	15-35/min.
Heart Rate	Approximately 220/min.
Urine Specific Gravity	1.006-1.017.
Kidney Function	Glomerular filtration increases from 21% at birth to 53% at 8 weeks of age. Tubular secretion rate matures at 8 weeks of age.
Sucking Reflex	Usually strong at birth. Weak in physically immature, abnormal, or chilled puppies.
Shivering Reflex	Develops 6-8 days after birth.
Muscle Tone	Firm; pups stand upright at 3 weeks with normal tone and postural reflexes. Walking and running by 4 weeks.
Eyes Open	10-16 days.
Visual Perception (owner recognition)	Absent less than 3 weeks; present at 4 weeks.
Hyperkinesia (body twitching)	Normal 1-3 weeks; disappears after 4 weeks.

WEANING

BY the time the babies are three weeks old they will begin to try and explore their environment. Life is no longer confined to eating and sleeping. They will enjoy being allowed to wander around outside their whelping box and may even become interested in relieving themselves on newspapers left directly outside their box. The mother will now leave them for longer periods of time and will hurry back merely to feed them. Sharp little teeth, as well as sharp little nails, which make their appearance at this time make nursing quite uncomfortable. Keep these trimmed and the bitch will be most grateful. Weaning is usually started at about four weeks of age and teaching the puppies to lap is the first lesson. Try using either infant formulae, Esbilac (substitute puppy milk), or mix up a combination of milk, cream, and a teaspoon of Karo Syrup. Offer the pups this in a shallow dish, but be prepared to encourage them by pushing their heads down a few times until they get the idea of how to eat from this new "dish." A week of milk nursing substitute beginning once a day and increased to four times a day is a good plan. Follow this the next few days with a milky mixture of pre-cooked baby cereal, enriched with a teaspoon of Karo Syrup and an egg yolk. At this point, your puppies should be eating heartily four times a day with the mother allowing them to nurse for only a few short times a day if at all. It is usually wise to give each pup his own pan of food in order to be certain that all are getting enough. Let them have as much as they want since this is the time of tremendous growth. Should you notice that one dog is monopolizing feeding time, then have him eat separately. Bitches will often regurgitate their own food to teach their pups to eat more solid food.

Usually by the fifth week, most pups are ready for a somewhat more substantial diet. If you have sufficient time to devote to the somewhat laborious task of preparing your own puppy food of cereal, eggs, and scraped meat or cooked hamburger, cottage cheese, enriched with vitamins, and you enjoy doing it then go ahead. On the other hand, if you can't afford the time or money required for this enterprise, then use a good quality puppy food starting at about six weeks. If fed moistened food, the pup should be fed three times a day until three to four months of age, then twice daily is adequate until he is eight to nine months of age. Feed all the moistened ration the pup will clean up at each feeding.

The period from weaning to approximately 20 weeks of age is the time when most pups grow fastest. During this period of rapid growth, medium-sized

Sharp teeth and nails make nursing quite uncomfortable as the pups grow older.

dogs, such as Pointer and Setters, require approximately three and one-half pounds of air-dry food to put on one pound of body weight gain. Larger breeds require slightly less, smaller breeds slightly more food per pound of gain. If canned dog foods are fed, three times as much canned food will normally be needed. Until the pups are about eight months old, they should have all the food they want.

When the pups are eight to ten weeks of age, they will consume the highest amount of feed in proportion to their body weight than at any other time in their lives except for lactating females. As the dog matures and gains weight, the amount of feed intake in proportion to body weight gradually decreases and levels off at maturity. If at any time during the growing period, the dog tends to become overweight, then his feed intake should be reduced.

Although most good quality commercial dog foods do contain vitamins and minerals in the suggested proportions, some veterinarians recommend adding vitamins and other additives. We would suggest you consult your own vet in this regard. A large and reputable dog food producer has the following to say about supplementing your dog's diet:

Many dog owners refuse to believe that good commercial dog foods contain all of the nutrients, except water, needed by normal dogs for all phases of their lives. Occasionally an individual dog may have a requirement for a particular nutrient that is higher than the average, but this is exceptional and is quite often the result of a metabolic abnormality.

Supplementation is costly, unnecessary and may cause nutritionally-induced physiological health problems. How can this happen?

Adding raw whole eggs to rations for puppies, or even mature dogs, is not uncommon. Raw egg white contains avidin, an enzyme, which ties up the vitamin, biotin, and if fed continually, a biotin deficiency can occur. Raw egg whites are used to produce biotin deficiencies experimentally. Symptoms include dermatitis, loss of hair, and poor growth. Although it is not necessary to add eggs to the diet, the addition of *cooked* eggs will not result in the destruction of biotin.

Adding supplemental minerals, such as calcium pills, to a regular diet can also be detrimental. It is known that both calcium and phosphorus must be present in the ration in ample amounts and in a proper ratio of 1.2:1 promotes maximum calcification. If additional calcium is added to make this ratio further apart, for example 5:1, there would be an inefficient assimilation of these two minerals even though the phosphorus was present in the correct amount. Rickets is one sign of a deficiency or imbalance of either of these two minerals in the diet of growing dogs.

Cod liver oil and wheat germ oil are sources of vitamins D and E. Adding excess cod liver oil can supply more vitamin D than is needed by the dog. Vitamin D must also be given in the proper proportion along with calcium and phosphorus for good bone and tooth formation.

If either of these two oils are in the process of becoming rancid, or if a rancid fat is added, this can destroy the vitamin E. In fact, low levels of rancid fish oil are often used to produce a vitamin E deficiency in experimental work. Vitamin E is needed for normal growth, reproduction, and lactation. All of the vitamins known to be required by normal dogs are added in sufficient quantities to most good commercial

Here's a litter of puppies enjoying a cafeteria style meal. Keeping them out of the food dish is quite a problem —one solution is to provide a small eating area.

dog foods. These vitamins are in stable forms and can withstand the heat and pressures that might occur during manufacturing and possible long periods of warehouse storage.

Many young puppies, especially prior to weaning, are fed a mixture of milk, baby cereal, vitamins, eggs, and meat. Besides being expensive, the preparation of a diet of this type is time-consuming and difficult. A good commercial dry dog food that has been moistened is highly palatable for pups and will supply them with the balanced nutrition that cannot be met by many home-mixes.

Occasionally charcoal is added to the diet. Unless fed in excessive amounts this ingredient is usually considered to be harmless, but there is no real advantage in using it. It is relatively indigestible and may take up some vitamins in the digestive tract and carry them out of the dog.

Hard-working dogs, such as racing Greyhounds, sled dogs and hunting dogs, require a high level of feed intake to meet their high-energy requirements. It is very important that they receive a highly palatable ration so they consume a high caloric intake. Many people add 20 to 25 per cent raw meat to the diet; this does not improve the nutritional balance of the ration but may increase acceptance. Meat fed at this level should not cause any problems. However, it is not advisable to feed extremely high levels of meat or only lean meat as the entire ration. Meat is deficient in certain minerals, including calcium, cobalt, iron and copper, as well as some vitamins. Young growing puppies fed only lean meat will develop severe rickets after being on this type diet for only three to four weeks. Meat is the only supplement we recommend adding to a dry dog food and this is only for normal dogs that have a high-energy requirement and need a food intake that is higher.

Supplementation is not necessary and may even prove to be detrimental at times. More and more dog owners are discovering that supplementation of a good commercial dog food offers no advantage for their dogs. This fact has been proven time and time again by the many thousands of dogs self-fed dry rations and water with excellent results.

Drinking water should be available at all times as puppies drink a lot and if only milk is offered it may be difficult later for them to adjust to water.

By the age of ten weeks regular milk can be used instead of the formula or enriched milk.

Try to feed your puppy on a schedule and be consistent in the hours. Here is a good schedule to follow:

Feeding Schedule

Age of Puppy	Morning	Noon	Evening
6 weeks to 6 months	X	X	X
6 months to a year	X		X
Past one year			X

Selling Puppies

By the age of eight weeks puppies are customarily offered for sale. Occasional breeders make it a rule to keep their pups until they are 12 weeks of age in order to give them an extra "good start." For the breeder, keeping the puppies longer involves added expense and care. Food, innoculations, grooming and attention are required. When the litter is large, this can become quite a strain physically as well as financially. It is for this reason that it is usual to find dogs for sale as soon as they are weaned and independent from their mother. Thus, when considering your sales program, try to be mindful of these elements and plan accordingly.

Advertising in the local paper, city newspapers and special dog magazines is one of the best ways of reaching the public. Since most dog magazines appear only once a month, you will have to place your ad well in advance. Much time will be saved if you are explicit in your ad. State the breed, number, age, sex and lineage as well as price of your puppies and include your phone number or address. Vague ads result in numerous unnecessary and fruitless inquiries.

Inform your vet, stud owner, and local pet store about your saleable puppies. These people constantly get inquiries and may be able to steer customers in your direction. Once your puppies are offered for sale be prepared to spend a great deal of time on the phone answering a flood of questions and a great deal of time showing your babies to prospective buyers. People purchasing a dog do not usually rush into it and may want to spend hours observing them. It may be necessary for you to give specific appointments including a cut-off time. However, one can't be overly rigid as making sales is the purpose.

Setting a fair price can be difficult. It will be necessary for you to inquire as to the going rates for the particular breed that you have. Many factors come into price consideration, such as:

1—Breed
2—Blood lines—ancestry
3—Championships
4—Sex
5—Age
6—Innoculations received
7—Surgery performed (dew claws, ears cropped, tails docked).

Weigh these elements carefully to determine a fair price. Your price must be in line with other puppies on the market. If yours are significantly lower, perhaps you are undervaluing your goods, and you are hurting the market. Should your price be too high, you probably won't be able to make a sale. Don't be surprised if selling all the puppies takes quite a while and be prepared for this possibility. Finding the right home is not the easiest event in the world and there may be occasions when you will refuse to sell to a party. Most real dog lovers won't allow their puppies to go to families or homes that don't meet certain standards. If you have to make such a decision, don't feel badly—it's probably the wisest thing. Puppies that you have raised will undoubtedly become very dear to you and their welfare should be one of your prime concerns.

Most sources agree that it is never wise to give a puppy away or to sell it too cheaply since too many people equate worth with price. Thus, if you want your pup to be highly valued, you must ask a fair price for it.

The Sale

Be prepared for the sale of your puppies; if they are pure bred dogs, this event should have been anticipated and the litter registered with the A.K.C. All the necessary forms and pedigrees should be ready for the new owner. It's also a good idea to have a mimeographed diet sheet including instructions on care and training. This prepared information can save time and misunderstanding. Here's a handy list for you to check off:

Getting Puppy Ready for New Home . . .

☐ Fecal sample checked for worms. Worm if necessary according to internal parasites present:
    Roundworms
    Hookworms
    Tapeworms
    Whipworms
    Heartworms (in blood samples—vet cannot detect in puppies less than 12 weeks of age.)
☐ Clip toe nails and dew claws (remove dew claws during the first week after birth).
☐ Check teeth.
☐ Clean eyes if they contain foreign matter.
☐ Trim excess hair from around anal and urinary openings.
☐ Bathe and clip, trim or pluck if necessary (generally not before 6 weeks of age).
☐ Consult your veterinarian and follow immunization or protective health program.
☐ Acclimatize dogs by careful display and handling.
☐ Provide new owners with guarantees that their new pet will be found healthy by a veterinarian.
☐ Supply new puppy owner with an information sheet describing care, feeding, management, and sanitation for the new puppy.
☐ Have registration certificate ready.

Persons buying a puppy will often ask to see the parents of the pup. If you don't own the stud, it is helpful to have a good photograph to show.

SHOWING

SHOWING

WHY show your dog? Without a doubt, most people show their dogs initially because they feel that their dog is a fine specimen of the breed and they wish others to see this as well. The competition of a show provides an excellent opportunity for dogs to be compared, contrasted, and evaluated. Win, lose, or draw —the show is always an educational experience for the owners as well as the spectators. Perhaps, the aftermath of a show will mean changes for your dog —better grooming, better training, or entry in other shows.

There is fun and excitement at a show and if your dog does make a good appearance you will be encouraged to pursue this endeavor. After several shows, who knows? You might even be ready to take this up as a hobby.

Showing Dogs—Quite a Hobby

Showing dogs can become a family hobby which is enjoyed by the members of all ages. Here is a hobby which has no special season—it goes on all year around. Dog fanciers can participate in this sport as much or as little as they desire. Many folks who show regularly state that their enthusiasm grows as they become more involved. First, they start with one dog, usually the family pet, and then if they are successful in their showing venture, they expand their enterprise. Attaining points for a champion is frequently the greatest incentive. Now, perhaps they will add an additional dog to the "family." If there are children, they will be indoctrinated by participating in the Junior Showmanship events. These junior shows give young people a chance to appear with their dog in front of an audience. They can develop poise and self-confidence through such participation.

Although there are costs and time involved, all the people we have queried feel that it's all worth it. They find that the closeness between the family is strengthened because of this joint enterprise. Any hobby involves expense and they find that showing requires no more than golf or bowling. A show is very exciting, challenging, and fun. Many also find it gives them an excuse to travel which they might otherwise not do. And, last but not least, this is an opportunity to meet and talk to many people and to exchange bits of interesting information and dog lore.

All in all, this is a hobby which many can enjoy and which you may find is just the thing for your family.

Showing—For a Serious Purpose

Should you desire to get involved with dogs somewhat seriously—let's say breeding or having a stud, or grooming—then the dog show exposure can give you valuable opportunities in (1) elevating your dog's status, (2) giving many people the opportunity to observe your dog, (3) giving you a chance to meet people interested in your services.

To learn where and when dog shows are held, write to the dog show superintendent and request that your name be placed on their mailing list; you will receive advance notice of the shows.

This dog show information which is sent is called the premium list. It will tell you the date of the show, the place, whether the show is benched or unbenched, and the amount of the entry fee. It will also give you the names of the judges, prizes, and when the last entries will be accepted. Should you decide to enter a show, send in the properly completed application with the required fee.

Showing can cost you a lot of money or it can be an inexpensive hobby. Hiring a professional handler to show your dog will be expensive, but he knows his trade and will present your dog at his best. Most dog owners handle their own dogs and, thus, can participate and enjoy all the excitement and if they win it is even more satisfying.

Preparing Your Dog for the Show
Training

The conformation class of a dog show is the opportunity for your dog to display his best physical qualities and his best performance. Thus, he must be groomed to make a fine appearance, and he must be trained in good conduct, for the judge will form his opinion based on what he sees—how the dog stands, walks, and runs.

Long before that exciting "first" show, you must train your dog to do the following:

1—Walk on the lead.

Holding the leash quite short, practice walking with the dog on your left side, training him to adjust to your speed and to stop when you stop. Conduct regular daily practice sessions which are fun, and yet instill pride and discipline.

2—Hold a pose.

Train your dog to allow you to pose him—to place him in the required stance position with the head up, alert expression, feet well-placed—thus displaying all his best features. Getting him used to this pose position from puppyhood to adulthood is good training.

3—Stand for examination.

In training your dog to allow the judge to examine him during a show, have friends examine him on a regular basis. This practice will help him to become accustomed to having his teeth checked and his body investigated.

Grooming

Trimming must be done weeks before a show. Hard coats grow more slowly than soft ones and thus must be started earlier. Until you are completely aware of the breed standards, your dog's assets and deficits, and are proficient in the proper grooming techniques, let a professional do the trimming. If you wish to eventually learn this aspect of dog care, then by all means analyze your dog's preparation and seek advice on how to do it. There are courses offered that can help you master this.

The night before the show is a good time for a bath if it is needed. Place the dog in a tub, wet his coat thoroughly with lukewarm water, apply dog shampoo, rub until thick and sudsy, massage starting at the neck and working back. Be sure to protect the eyes and ears. Use a spray to rinse until all soap is out. Dry well by using a dryer or thick towel. Brush out and pin a towel around the dog with large safety pins.

The day of the show, check the time your dog will be in the ring and gauge your grooming accordingly. You will want to allow ample time to brush, comb, and tidy up your dog but still not start too early so that he is wilted long before entering the ring.

Smooth, short-coated dogs need merely to be rubbed down with a grooming glove and if the coat needs a shine, rub on just a little hair cream.

Long, flat coats should be sponged to remove dust and then brushed well.

Terriers should not be bathed more than necessary as it softens their hard coat. White terriers can be chalked to clean and whiten the coat but this chalk must be brushed out thoroughly before the judging.

Light colored poodles can be powdered, but this must all be completely brushed out prior to entering the show ring.

Towels should be used to protect dogs that drool. Protect the long-eared dogs from soiling themselves while eating.

At your first few shows, observe the professional handlers. They are usually glad to share some of their knowledge with you.

How to Behave the Day of the Show

Don't tire or overexcite your dog. The trip, the new surroundings, the crowd, and the other dogs are all terribly exciting so try to instill a calm element by remaining as relaxed and as natural as possible. Nervousness is contagious and could hurt your dog's showing, so exercise self-control.

Let your dog rest as much as possible and do only the necessary grooming. Allow him to eat and relieve himself according to his normal schedule, if possible. Some authorities recommend feeding long before the judging so that the dog is more spirited and not sluggish after a heavy meal.

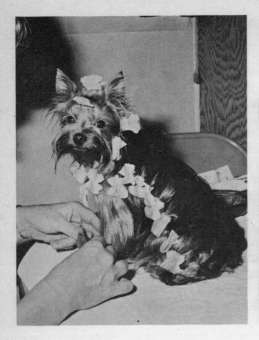

Left—A Yorkshire Terrier must go through elaborate preparations prior to a show. This is an example of how the Yorky looks after an oil spray and wrapping to preserve a good show coat. Below—Getting this dog's coat into show condition is going to be quite a chore.

The judging schedule will explain the time and ring in which your dog is to appear. Be on time as they will start without you if you are not there. Upon arrival at the ring, the attendant will give you an arm band bearing the entry number of your dog. This band is to be worn on the left arm.

When the group of dogs enters the ring, all the dogs are to be on their handlers' left side. Keep an eye on the judge and listen to his commands. Never block the judge's view of your dog. Try to keep your dog moving or posed while in the ring and have a special toy or treat in your hand to keep his attention.

Pose your dog carefully and be sure to allow yourself plenty of room. Place the forelegs so that they stand correctly; pull the head forward and up as you hold the tail in proper position.

When the judge makes his decision, accept it gracefully. Should you be a winner, that's fine. But, if your dog doesn't place in the winners' circle, please maintain a pleasant attitude. Judges try to make their selections fairly and carefully and their decisions should not be contested. If you wish to discuss your dog and get a candid opinion on how to improve his chances, most judges will be glad to talk to you briefly after the group is finished, when time permits. Dog shows are competitive and one must be prepared to lose as well as to win. As with any sport, it's how you play the game that counts. Enjoy the preliminary preparations and the show itself, and, then, winning needn't be so terribly important.

Professional Handlers

Many dogs are shown by professional handlers. About 1,000 handlers are licensed by the American Kennel Club. A professional handler is one who may board and train a dog to show, and, then, show it for the owner. For this, he charges a fee agreed upon for that show. Professional handlers may take many dogs to a single show. Professional handlers often arrange to take "strings" of dogs on "circuits" — a half-dozen or more shows held in towns and cities fairly close together so that the dogs and handlers move from one to another quite easily. For example, there are the Deep South Circuit, the Florida Circuit, the South Texas Circuit, etc.

Some professional handlers have full time jobs and go only to weekend dog shows. These handlers simply accept their clients' dogs at the shows. They bathe, trim and groom them, and then take them into the ring; whereas others own large kennels and board dogs for the general public as well.

Things to Remember

1—If the dog is having skin trouble or is out of coat, don't show him.

2—Be sure all innoculations against distemper, hepatitis, and leptospirosis are up to date.

3—Items to bring to the show for your dog are: collar and bench chain; show lead; dog food and water dish; comb, brush, sponge, towel, and all necessary grooming preparations.

4—Items to bring to the show for your own needs are: a folding chair; any refreshments you need and don't want to buy; paper and pencil to take notes; comfortable clothing with roomy pockets.